Nuked at the Prom

Reid is an astrologer, one of the U.K.'s top hand
sts and a prolific writer of bestselling books for adults
ildren on dreams and related subjects. As an expert
field she is regularly featured on radio and television
e U.K., and her weekly astrological column is
ated in both national and international newspapers.

Naked at the Prom

The Secret Language of Dreams

Lori Reid

Ulysses Press

Published by   Ulysses Press
              P.O. Box 3440
              Berkeley CA 94703
              www.ulyssespress.com

ISBN 1-56975-356-3
Library of Congress Control Number 2003104412

First published in the United Kingdom in 2002 by Rider,
an imprint of Ebury Press, Random House

Illustrations by Rob Loxston

Printed in Canada by Transcontinental Printing

10 9 8 7 6 5 4 3 2 1

Distributed in the United States by Publishers Group West
and in Canada by Raincoast Books

Contents

Acknowledgements

A big thank you to all those who over the years have shared their dreams and experiences with me. But my very special thanks go to Shirley Wallis, my friend, teacher and guide, who gave me so much of her time and valuable help in the writing of this book.

Introduction

Whether they're weird or wonderful, simple or complex, funny or terrifying, our dreams are, without doubt, totally fascinating.

Everybody dreams. Some people claim they never do, but the fact is they just don't remember! It's been estimated that if a person lives to the grand old age of 75, they will have slept for an amazing total of 25 years. And during those 25 years, they will have spent something like 50,000 hours deep in dreamland.

Research has shown that young people dream considerably more than older folk do, and babies dream the most. On average, a teenager can dream for as long as four or five hours each night, while a 40-year-old is lucky to get as much as 90 minutes' worth.

Interestingly, animals dream, too. You may have noticed it yourself when your pets quiver and growl in their sleep, probably dreaming of climbing trees or chasing rabbits down holes. Certainly, scientists tell us that dreaming is essential to our health and well-being because our dreams act as safety valves, releasing frustrations, anxieties and

feelings. But dreams can do more than that. As we sleep, they form the vital link between our conscious and subconscious minds, carrying important messages to us about our waking lives.

Centuries of study and research into dreams have revealed the importance of dreaming. It is believed that our dreams:

- organize and make sense of events that occur during the day, bringing to light the things that bother us the most. This is a valuable safety valve in our lives.

- can point the way to solving problems, showing us how to overcome difficulties and obstacles with inspired solutions.

- alert us to situations or information we might otherwise have missed.

- sort out past events and clear unnecessary memories and feelings, thus preparing us for the next day, the immediate future and, sometimes, the long-term future, too.

- restore our physical and mental balance.

- allow us to play out our fantasies, longings and desires, thus providing fun and light relief.

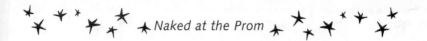

The amazing thing is that all of this activity carries on whether we're conscious of it or not! When you become more aware of the mechanics of dreaming, you can begin to see the benefits more clearly and you can even teach yourself to make your dreams work for you. Don't forget, you are the dreamer, the dreaming and the dream all rolled up into one incredible human being.

Once you get the hang of it you can have more say in the type of dreams you have – and can even control what goes on in those dreams. It's like being a film-maker. You are your own producer and director, deciding what goes into your film and very often taking the starring role, too!

Turn to the Lucid Dreaming section on page 119 to find out more about creating your own blockbuster movie dream and how that can help you to sort out problems in your everyday life.

Talking to yourself

Throughout your life, parts of you are always talking to each other. The part of your mind in charge of dreaming is a major department in your vast organization of personal communications. You are always logged on whether you are awake, daydreaming, dozing or sleeping. You are con-

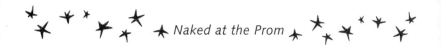

stantly processing information that you receive through your senses. As a person, you are state of the art and as unique as your fingerprints. The things that you experience outwardly in your day-to-day or conscious life are stored in various areas of your mind. Mainly, these caches of files are located in the subconscious regions of your brain. Your conscious and subconscious are constantly in dialogue, holding conversations with each other, sifting, filing, linking and cross-referencing data to prevent your system from going into mental and emotional overload.

During the day, when you want to remember something you send a signal to the memory department, and if you want to be really sure you might even write yourself a note on a Post-it and stick it on your mirror, or write it on your hand, or jot it down in a planner. In other words, what you're doing is bringing the signal out into the open (or "into consciousness") because you want to be sure that you won't forget – something that can easily happen if your attention is suddenly diverted or you encounter a stressful situation during your day.

If you want to make a note of something when you're asleep, you also send a message from your subconscious to your conscious mind. That note is called a dream. It may be a simple impression of the day, a conversation you had with a friend, a piece of information you learned, events or observations or perhaps some advice to yourself – a com-

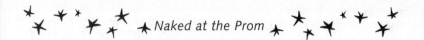

ment or encouragement for something you plan to do. But just as there are all sorts of notes you could write – reminders to take your library book back, phone numbers to put into your address book, a saying that's inspired you, a list of stuff to take to school tomorrow or a love note – so there are all sorts of dreams.

Types and themes of dreams

Dream researchers have found that there are several common types of dreams, which vary according to the sort of information being processed. Some are the "tidying up" kind, some are reminders, some give us answers to questions and some can even give us clues to the future. Here are the most common types:

Factual dreams

Factual or "residual" dreams are not usually laden with meaning and messages that need lots of analysis and interpretation. They tend to be memories in picture form, replaying something that took place during the day, recording an event or even a person you met. They are bits and pieces that occur as part of a sorting and filing process.

Sometimes a factual dream can enhance a sensation. If while dreaming you are using your senses, this gives you a wider knowledge of your waking (conscious) sensing skills. For example, if your doorbell rings or your alarm goes off while you're dreaming, you might weave that sound into your dream so that it becomes a fire engine rushing to a blaze. Cooking smells wafting from the kitchen into your bedroom might be incorporated into a dream banquet. These types of factual dreams are called "vigilant" dreams. They show that although you may be asleep, your brain continues to receive and process information from your senses.

Creative and wish-fulfilling dreams

Creative dreams can be inspirational. They can provide the answers to problems and solutions to dilemmas in your waking life. A creative dream can show the exact way, the place, the idea that you've been looking for.

Sam's dream

Sam's ambition was to go to college and study jour-nalism. To qualify for admission he needed a high SAT II score in French. Unfortunately, he was strug-gling and was bitterly disappointed when he received a low score on a practice exam. He was so upset that he started to have nightmares. His mother became worried and suggested finding him a private

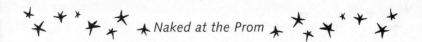

tutor. It took only a few lessons for Sam to see he was making good progress, but the real break-through came after the fourth week when he had a dream that boosted his confidence. In the dream he was sitting with his tutor, books open on the table in front of him. But the writing was a jumble of indeci-pherable scribble. Just then, he looked out of the window and caught sight of the clouds parting and the sun suddenly shining through against a brilliant blue sky. Turning back to his books he discovered that he could now read the writing perfectly.

This dream was confirming that Sam was making good progress with his French and the extra lessons were helping him to "see the light." Whereas before he was confused, now he was able to read, write and understand the language far better.

This kind of dream can feel very real and exhilarating. It can leave you feeling happy and satisfied. It's the sort of dream that can spur you on to success, providing the magical for-mula that will enable you to fulfill your ambitions. In fact, this dream often unlocks latent talents that have yet to be recognized. It also proves that our subconscious does the creative work if we give it the space to do so.

Problem-solving dreams

Writers and inventors, scientists and engineers – in fact, all kinds of people from every walk of life – have solved some of their most important problems or had inspiration for their work through dreaming while awake!

The old saying "I'll sleep on it" before coming to a final decision on something is one of the wisest statements. Even if you received no obvious dream or mind-blowing answer during the night, you might find that after one of these dreams you feel differently when you wake up in the morning. Dream-time has created some space for you, where your mind can become more objective. You may not even notice the subtle changes that have taken place, but something has happened … and you just know what to do. Problem-solving dreams are in some ways similar to creative dreams.

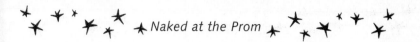

Nightmares

Dream researchers have found that regular nightmares are more commonly experienced by children and young people, but anyone of any age can have one. Nightmares come in varying degrees of intensity. You've probably had that classic one where you're being chased but your legs get heavier and heavier and just refuse to work! Monsters are growling or making awful noises, you're under attack, someone has a knife or a gun, you're terrified, you try to find somewhere to hide. Then suddenly you're falling into blackness and you wake up just before you hit the ground! Your heart is pounding, you're covered in sweat and trembling as you reach for the light switch. It's just another bad dream but it can still take a while for you to calm down because it seemed so real.

After a nightmare, it's always a good idea to change the subject by getting a drink, reading something calming or going to the bathroom. However, if you want to think about it so you can interpret the dream later, you must record/write down the key elements at once and as best you can (see Keeping a Dream Diary on page 20).

Nightmares are the result of inner fears or anxieties that have been triggered off by something – perhaps by a horror movie before bed, anxiety about upcoming tests, a serious problem you don't know how to handle, or even just being scared of someone or something. But not all nightmares are

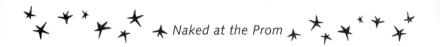
caused by fears in your waking life. Many are due to physical factors; a fever when you're not well can cause a nightmare, as can eating a big meal late at night.

Matt's dream

One night, Matt dreamed that he was trapped on the face of a gigantic clock. The hands, heavy and black, were spinning fast and chasing him so that he had to run for his life, around and around the clock, because if the hands caught him he would be crushed to death.

Curiously, Matt was a terrible time-keeper, always sleeping through the alarm and always late for school. He had this disturbing dream the night after a harsh lecture from his teacher for his constant tardiness. So, not only did he get a reprimand from his teacher, but he was told off by his subconscious, too!

— ❧ —

Prophetic and Precognitive Dreams

You might dream about a train or plane crashing or some other kind of national disaster. Then later the same day, or perhaps the next or even a week later, when you hear a report on the radio or see such an event on television, you realize that it's all happened before in your dream!

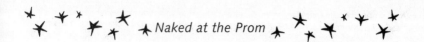

The classic example of a prophetic dream was the one Joseph had warning of the severe famine that was to befall Egypt. Fortunately, the Pharaoh listened to Joseph and took immediate action. He began to store food through the years of plenty and so avoided starvation during the leaner times when crops failed.

In more recent times, there have been instances of prophetic dreams giving warnings of forthcoming disasters. Many people, for example, dreamed about the sinking of the Titanic, and have foreseen volcanic eruptions and the assassination of well-known people such as President Kennedy and Martin Luther King, Jr. The information given in such dreams doesn't prevent the actual event, but often dreamers do act on these intuitive dreams or messages. Some decided not to travel on the Titanic, for example. And you hear of people who have cancelled a flight because of a foreboding dream. However, these prophetic dreams very rarely come true, and even when a disaster does happen there is usually a rational explanation for it.

Not all precognitive dreams are about disasters and calamities. Some actually foretell good fortune; several lottery winners have admitted that the winning numbers came to them in their sleep.

Ben's dream

Ben is an avid reader and every Saturday he and his father go to their local library and spend an hour together happily browsing through the books. So it wasn't surprising for Ben to have a dream set in a library. In his dream, Ben saw his father taking a book off the shelf and happened to notice that the title was *How To Make a Million*. His dad opened the book and, to their astonishment, out poured a stream of shiny, gold coins.

The very next Saturday, Ben's father won the lottery.

— ✄ —

Recurring dreams

A dream that recurs is trying to attract your attention to something that needs sorting in your life. It's very important that you carefully write down this dream every time it occurs. If you do, you'll be able to spot any variations from one dreamtime to the next, which will give you clues as to how things in your waking life are developing.

Recurring dreams are really those that have the same scenery, the same place and the same action. You may

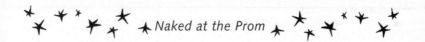

always be the observer in the dream, or you may always be taking part in the never-changing action.

This type of dream may only appear from time to time, but it can repeat itself throughout your lifetime. After a while you may be aware of subtle developments in the dream, such as more detail in a familiar scene. But this is likely to be just your subconscious feeding information through bit by bit so as not to overload the circuit.

An interesting suggestion as to why some dreamers have recurring dreams has come from people who research the possibility of past lives. They have said that this type of dream may be a cameo of a previous existence, a memory that has lingered on for some reason – and this is what the dreamer needs to work out.

Out-of-the-body experiences (OOBEs)

You may have noticed that sometimes when you're asleep you get the sensation of rising up towards the ceiling and then looking down on your resting body. This isn't strictly a type of dream, but because it involves the feeling that you're floating (which can develop into dream flying), the similarity is worth noting.

This experience is far more common than is generally thought, but people are often reluctant to talk about it. It's not really a big deal except that it helps you to realize once

again that you are so much more than just a physical body. These sensations of freedom are brilliant and normal and you should try not to be scared about the idea if you haven't already experienced an OOBE. While it's actually happening, you'll find it all quite natural and not at all alarming.

Sometimes hospital patients have reported having an OOBE where they watched their own operation and even heard what the surgeon was saying!

Unfortunately, all too often when people who have experienced an OOBE try to explain what's happened, others are dismissive and say the whole thing was a dream. This tends not only to belittle the OOBE but also to devalue the importance of dreams and dreaming as a whole.

Here comes the science

Researchers who have been studying sleeping and dreaming have discovered that there are different levels of sleep. To actually fall asleep takes about 10–15 minutes, during which time you drift through a kind of twilight phase of hazy pictures and increasing muscle relaxation as your limbs feel heavier and heavier. It's at this stage that you sometimes feel yourself suddenly falling and involuntarily jolt

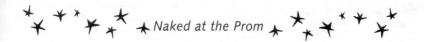

yourself back awake. Scientifically, this is known as a "myoclonic jerk" and it is believed to happen when either blood pressure falls or body temperature decreases.

As you settle down again, you begin to sink through different stages, from light sleep into deeper sleep and then to very deep sleep. It's here that you are at your most relaxed, and trying to wake you would take some considerable effort. From this very deep sleep you begin to rise up through the levels again until you reach the top level of lighter sleep once more. And it's at this point that you start to dream.

In all, this sinking and rising – from light down to very deep and back up to light sleep – takes roughly 90 minutes, and it's a process that repeats itself over and over until you finally wake up the next morning. During an average night's sleep, you may pass through five or six of these complete cycles.

Throughout these different stages, your body's responses change, too. The most interesting response takes place when you are dreaming. If someone watches you they'll notice that your eyeballs move rapidly beneath your closed eyelids, almost as if you were watching a movie at a theater. This is known as Rapid Eye Movement (REM), and during this stage dreaming is clear, active and like a magical picture show. Researchers can actually measure how long a dream lasts by timing the duration of REM movements.

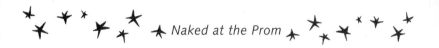
Non-rapid eye movement (NREM) describes the deeper levels of sleep when no true dreaming takes place. Throughout the night we alternate between these two states, with the deep sleeping stage getting shallower and the REM period getting longer, until the last 20–40 minutes before waking. The dreams you have at this point in your sleep are those you are most likely to recall and which, it seems, tend to carry the most important messages of all. To sleep or not to sleep?

Some experiments have shown that if we are deprived of sleep, the next time we get the chance to hit the sack we will spend more time in REM sleep, suggesting a kind of catching up. This tends to emphasize how important dreaming is and how essential it is for our general health.

During World War II, sleep deprivation was used as a form of torture. Prisoners were forced to stay awake by being made to walk, take cold showers or listen to loud music. This was one way to crack their resistance to questioning,

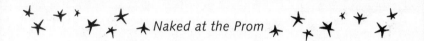

and as a result, many suffered severe personality disorders and some even died.

Because sleeping and dreaming are so crucial, our brains sometimes demand the sleep they need for their regeneration – which is why we can suddenly doze off in a boring lecture or the hum of a car engine can lull us into sleep.

We talk about "snatching 40 winks" or having a "cat nap." This is very beneficial and, if necessary, can keep you going over long periods of time. So don't be inhibited, just remember you are processing. And if you can get those eyes closed under suitable circumstances, do so – perchance to dream!

The language of dreams

When we interpret our dreams, it's like cracking a code. If you've ever wondered why our dreams are like riddles or puzzles it's because the information they contain is presented to us in a language made up of images and symbols. It may all seem complicated and confusing, sometimes even downright frustrating, but in actual fact it's just a form of shorthand that the mind uses to simplify the message.

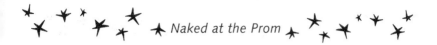

There's a difference between images and symbols. Images are personal to you, they're your own thoughts, ideas, or feelings turned into a series of pictures like ordinary scenes in daily life. For example, if you were going through a rather confusing time in your waking life, you could describe it as "not being able see the forest for the trees," and you might have a dream where you're wandering around lost in a dark forest.

Other images that you weave into your dreams might involve your own pets, your parents or your house – people and things that you know. Your fears and feelings, too, come out in your dreams. A monster, for example, may represent a person you're having trouble with, or an idea that frightens you.

Symbols are slightly different because these are pictures that are common to everyone, or that at least can be universally recognized, like the sun, for example, which everyone would instantly associate with heat, light and summertime.

Some symbols can present a wealth of information. For instance, take your astrological sign. That simple picture of Taurus the Bull or Pisces the Fish represents pages and pages of characteristics and facts about a person belonging to that sign. In the same way, planetary symbols, company logos, secret codes, traffic signs and computer icons, to name a few, also contain all sorts of information in a single picture.

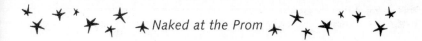

Often, symbols can have more than one meaning. A "cat" may be your beloved pet, but to describe somebody as a "cat" is quite a different story! These are the metaphorical symbols that are the most interesting in dreams because their complexity of meaning gives us insights into the subconscious – the way a person ticks deep down.

Our subconscious minds use imagery and symbols from our memory databank to relay meanings, dipping into old memory files and then linking with something that may have happened recently in waking life and presenting this whole package as a dream – perhaps for our attention or just to observe briefly what's happening and what's going on. It's all a kind of mind maintenance thing.

So, to unravel all those bits and pieces of your dream sequences – colors, numbers, shapes, people, situations, images and symbols – you need to shift your perceptions and approach. But always, and most importantly, you must recall the feelings you were experiencing in the dream because these will give you the main clues to the interpretation.

Don't forget, your dreams are made up of all your very own experiences, unique in depth, knowledge and emotion. These are mostly based on how you have experienced your waking life thus far. Therefore, only you can really interpret your dreams because you are the only expert on yourself!

Having said that, it doesn't mean that you know everything about yourself. Hidden talents are still tucked away, as well as many memories, both pleasant and unpleasant, that have been stored away since you were tiny. You may consciously have forgotten them, but subconsciously they are still there in the filing cabinet that is your mind.

It is this inside knowledge that you have to bring to the interpretation of your dreams.

Keeping a dream diary

If you truly want to work with your dreams you need to focus on them as they happen – which means keeping a simple record. Initially, you will forget most of your dreams as soon as you wake up. Fragments may remain, and dreams that have an emotional impact may stay with you for longer, but for the most part your dreams vanish the minute waking life kicks in. So don't trust your memory and hope for the best. If you want to take your dreams seriously, learn to keep a diary. You'll be amazed at how your recollections gradually improve and your awareness and observation of your inner surroundings develop as you progress.

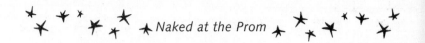

To keep a dream record, just follow these essential guidelines:

- A notebook and pencil beside the bed are a must. As soon as you wake from a dream, write it down.

- Always make a note of the date and then, if you can, write out the dream sequence in the order in which it happened. (This is more important than you may think because there are subtle links in a dream.) Was there anything recurring about the dream, any repeats of a previous dream?

- Describe the location of the dream with as much detail as you can. (You may have started out in a familiar spot you know in your waking life but then it quickly changed.)

- Record the people. Do you know them? If so, write down their names. If they were strangers to you, describe them. Were they well known or celebrities? Have you met them personally in your waking life or did they just appear in your dream? Did they remind you of someone you know? Did they have faces or was the face hidden?

- Describe anything non-human, such as animals, insects, monsters, aliens, angels, etc.

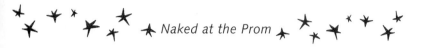

- Make a note of the colors and any patterns you saw. Did you hear sounds, such as voices, shouting, music, wind rushing, bells, etc.?

- What did you feel when you were dreaming? Were you frightened, angry, happy, excited? What do you feel now when you recall the dream?

- Do you already know/realize what the message of the dream was about?

Having recorded your dream, no matter how bizarre or silly it seemed as you wrote it down, you are now ready to analyze and try to understand the hidden codes and sort out the meaning or meanings, since there may be several levels all woven together.

Try to associate your dreaming with what is happening in your life right now. Are you worried about something like an exam, or about a person you love, or a family situation that's upsetting you? Could it be that you are longing for something, seeking an opportunity, or have you just had a fight with your best friend? When you're recording a dream try to keep in your mind what is happening in your real life and jot down some notes about that. This will help to clarify what's going on in your mind and help you interpret your dream.

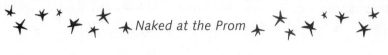

Associations
and links

The dreamworld can be perplexing, a place where things are upside-down, quickly changing from one thing to another, a place where you know who the person is in front of you yet it doesn't really look like them, or you know you're in your kitchen, yet it doesn't quite look the same as the one in real life.

It is important to note any quick changes since they can be important and informative links between one scene and another. Find a few words to describe each happening.

Sayings and proverbs can have associations that can be taken literally as they are played out dramatically in your dream. For example, you may have a prophetic weather dream where it's literally "raining cats and dogs," or you see "too many cooks in the kitchen," meaning you should be acting on your own ideas in waking life without so much interference from others.

There are also superstitions that can be played out in your dream. For instance, you may dream of a big black cat crossing your path. Now this dream may be a warning that the kitten at the pet shop you've been longing to buy isn't

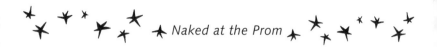

such a good idea. Or, on a different level, it could be telling you that a new and unexpected obstacle will be coming your way.

Song titles are also good ammunition for your "dream self" to use in order to convey information. Many people have a song running through their head as they wake up. If that happens to you, try to remember the words, since the message may be contained in the lyrics!

Names are often used as song titles so be on the alert for them, too, as well as first names in general. They are sometimes used as a sort of trick – the name William, for example, can be split up into Will-I-Am to convey someone who's being a bit too bossy towards you in waking life.

With a little practice, you'll soon get the hang of interpreting your dreams. If you get stuck or need to doublecheck anything, look it up in the following Secret Language of Dreams from A–Z. This should prompt your memory and help you to decode the mysteries of your nighttime reveries.

The Secret Language of Dreams from A-Z

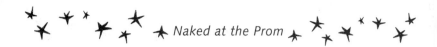

Accidents

With this dream, it's very important that you look carefully at the details – the location, the people and the role they play in the dream. Is there machinery? Are tools or vehicles involved? Do you perhaps trip or fall over something? Accidents imply carelessness, a need to take more care, or to watch out for mistakes. If people in the dream cause your accident, who are they? Someone in your waking life could be trying to stop you from going somewhere, or prevent you from doing something. Or this dream might be a warning for your own good. If you are in or on a vehicle that you can't stop, it could be suggesting that something in your life is out of control. Are you going too fast and neglecting details? The location will give the clues as to where the problem is rooted – at home, work, school, college. If, however, the accident occurs in a place you don't recognize, perhaps the implication is that things in your waking life are getting out of control, and the dream is showing you that you're afraid you might not be able to cope.

Acrobats

Are you the acrobat in your dream, or are you merely watching a troop of professionals? Taking part in acrobatics

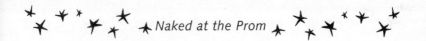

indicates display, getting a buzz or showing off. You could be "bending over backwards" to please someone or feel you're being forced into doing something against your nature. Watching a display in a dream is a form of admiration – it's thrilling and different. Do you have a desire in your waking life to do something that others are doing? Are you longing to succeed, wanting to be noticed or craving adventure? The art of balance can come into this type of dream, too, so take the "balancing act" into account if you are "in limbo" with a situation that's going on in your life.

Airplanes

A plane trip indicates a move towards independence, freedom, and leaving home and friends – flying away, leaving the nest. Waiting for the plane to take off, being stuck at the airport or delayed, means frustration – you're going nowhere. If you're the pilot, then you're in control of things. If you are a passenger and there is turbulence and flight problems, then be warned. Things are getting bumpy and out of control. Perhaps you need to take another look at what's happening in your life.

Aliens

If you dream of aliens you could just be releasing your fears after seeing a movie or television show, but note the circumstances in the dream because they refer to your waking

life and the word "alien." Are you at present in a place or situation that you don't understand or with which you feel uncomfortable? What is happening to make you anxious, confused or uncertain? If the dream is helpful, then it indicates an opportunity to explore the mysteries of life or perhaps find out more about the cosmos.

Alleyways

Is the alley dark and scary? Can you see a light at the end so you know where you're going? Are you walking or running? Alleyways indicate how you view your life right now. If you come to a dead end, that speaks for itself. If you're looking for a way out, perhaps you suddenly find an escape route. Is it a doorway that suddenly opens, or a crack that's hard to crawl though? This will indicate that there are answers if you search for them. But notice how much effort it takes to get out. That's important. Squeezing through an opening indicates pressure to get something done. If you are in despair and trapped, and your dream turns into a nightmare, do you yell for help and wake yourself up? This is your answer to what may seem an insurmountable problem. Your subconscious is telling you that you should ask someone for advice in waking life. (See also Tunnels and Lights.)

Arcades

This dream indicates fun and diversion. It shows that your

life is more relaxed and things are going well, especially if you're winning. If you're losing and feeling disappointed and frustrated it could be a warning that you're getting into a no-win situation in real life. It's suggesting that carrying on as you are is fruitless. It's asking you to think about your timing and to recognize when it's right to keep going and when it's appropriate to quit.

Angels

Angels are messengers. They appear with special information for you from deep within your subconscious. This could be important news of things to come, or information conveying comfort and protection. It could be that your very own guardian angel is appearing to reassure you that he/she is by your side. This dream is extra-special if it comes at a time when you're feeling lost, lonely or confused in some way. An angel is a symbol of love, peace and joy, so to dream of one indicates success and happiness. The appearance of an angel in a dream may also mean that the answer you're looking for is on its way.

Animals

Generally, animals reflect your basic reactions and instincts. Different animals represent different characteristics: someone you don't like very much may appear as a pig, whereas a comforting friend might be in the form of a cuddly kitten

or puppy. Another way of understanding a dream containing animals is to think of yourself as the animal you see and then recall the feelings you experienced in the dream. This could be helpful if you recognize the particular strength associated with that animal, maybe this is the characteristic your subconscious is suggesting you need to adopt. A lion, for example, is a cue for bravery, a dog for faithfulness. An animal can also come into a dream as a warning. A fox (indicating cunning) circling around you could be an indication that you need to be more wary of someone you know in real life. Sometimes your own pet appears in a dream, bringing comfort and loyalty, perhaps at a time when you need reassurance.

Babies

Babies symbolize new ideas. They also represent gifts and talents that have hidden potential. How does the baby appear to you in your dream? If you just see a baby or are handed one, this could mean that it's time to get started on the new project you've been thinking about, or something new is about to happen! Giving birth means you're ready to start. Finding a baby, on a doorstep, say, means you're going to find something new. But what are your feelings and reactions in the dream at this discovery? If you're dis-

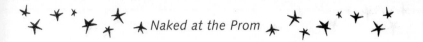

tressed or horrified, or the baby is crying or tiny, this "some-thing new" could well be difficult. Perhaps you need to think your ideas through, be practical and pay more attention to detail. New babies bring new experiences, so don't give up – concentrate and you'll soon discover the joys and blessings your life has to offer.

Bags

Bags, baggage, suitcases, backpacks, handbags – all kinds of luggage fall into the category of containers into which you put your work and belongings, so once again it's important to consider how these items appear in your dream. If you are carrying heavy baggage, what is your real-life burden? Is it yours or someone else's? Are you feeling overburdened at this time in your life? Did you get rid of or dump your heavy bag in the dream? All these questions refer to the responsibilities that you feel are a bit of a drag right now. If you open a bag and find valuables such as money or jew-elry, your dream is presenting good fortune, something of value like skills and talents, all coming "out of the bag"! If something horrible comes out of the bag, then obviously this is a warning. Something hidden is about to be revealed. You could be packing a bag in your dream and this can refer to hiding things, setting things aside that you don't want now or you don't want to deal with. Or it may simply mean you're about to go on a trip. To some dream specialists, a bag can be the symbol of a woman's uterus or vagina, so

there could be a sexual meaning here, especially if other images in the dream are erotic. If so, look under Sex for further information.

Balls/ball games

If you're playing with others in a team game like football, basketball or soccer, the dream is telling you about how well you're getting along with others like friends and family. This dream is about cooperating with others, so what happens, whether you're winning or losing or scoring goals, indicates how well you're doing right now in a group situation. Are you in a win-win situation or not? As a point scorer you may be wish-fulfilling, but it shows that you can accomplish something in real life right now. Expect some praise or success soon. You might be feeling really good about yourself and your dream is emphasizing your popularity. On the other hand, if you miss the goal you could feel you're letting others down in a real-life situation, perhaps feeling guilty about your part in the "game of life." Playing with a ball on your own – kicking or hitting it against a wall for instance – indicates that you might be lonely, or need to do your own thing at the moment, because you need to think about your next move in life. On another level, we call male testicles balls, so a dream of this kind may have a sexual meaning, especially if you see two balls together, like golf balls lying on a green or tennis balls on a court. If you're female, the

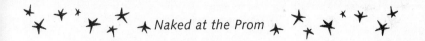

reference may be to a boy you know or someone you would like to get to know better. (See also Sex.)

Bathrooms

On a very basic level, dreaming about a bathroom may be a physical nudge to get up and use one! Dreaming that you're on a toilet in a public place is an embarrassment dream revealing that you're feeling vulnerable at the moment and may have a fear of being "found out" about something or other. Bathrooms are functional places for getting rid of matter, so the dream could be hinting that it's time you cleared out the clutter in your life. This can range from clearing old or unwanted things from your room to saying goodbye to unnecessary relationships or bad habits. (See also Embarrassment.)

Beaches

We usually associate the beach or seaside with vacations – a fun time when everyone is more relaxed. A beach dream often refers to "getting away from it all" – so what are you doing in your dream? If you are alone, peacefully looking out to sea, it could mean you're ready to start afresh or tackle a new challenge, especially if the sea is calm. A stormy scene, with big waves crashing towards you, means that emotional matters are your concern. This is because water in our dreams is often linked to our feelings. Beach

scenes in general are recreational and revitalizing, so the message refers to your creative talents coming out, being warmed and nurtured by the sun. This dream is most reassuring, telling you that things are looking really bright for you just now.

Bears

A bear appearing in a dream could refer to someone you know in real-life as "grizzly" or bad-tempered. Alternatively, this could be pointing to a big, cuddly person – a "bear" of a man or a teddy-bear type. If you see a real teddy bear, it may be a signal back to your childhood when you needed comfort. Perhaps a cuddle is what you really need now. If you are the bear in the dream, ask yourself if you've been acting like a grizzly bear recently. Bears can be magical, however; they can appear as messengers or guardians telling you that a new phase is coming into your life. This dream, then, is giving you strength, health and the ability to go ahead with confidence.

Bees

Are you "busy as a bee" in real life or is this a prompt from your Dream Self to stop messing around and get your act together? Bees and other insects are known for their industrious and organized nature, so they could simply be telling you that there's a busy time ahead that will be creative and

productive. Beware if you're stung in the dream – this is a warning, a sign of treachery foretelling that someone could let you down! Long ago, bees were said to be a symbol of good fortune, happiness and plenty, and people made a point of "telling the bees" the latest family news. They regarded the bees as messengers between our world and the Great Mother Universe.

Bells

Ringing bells mean news. In a dream they seek your attention. The type of peal gives the clue as to their message, because peals of bells can be joyful whereas a single bell tolling may be gloomy, possibly announcing news of a death. Or this bell could be summoning you to make an urgent visit. Alarm bells such as a fire alarm and your own alarm clock going off in real life are, of course, grabbing your attention. Sometimes, these can be incorporated into a dream just before you wake, but it's still important to take note of the scenario in which the ringing occurs since it may be alerting you to an impending situation. If you only see the bell without hearing its ring, think of the actual word

itself. Perhaps it's referring to someone you know with the last name Bell, or with the first name Bel or Bella. Generally, however, bells suggest you could be hearing some good news soon.

Boats

Sailing vessels of all kinds, from the smallest dinghy to the largest ship, are classed as a form of transport and any movement over land or water in dream lore represents the progress you're making in life. Gentle journeys over a calm sea or waterway show all is well. It's "smooth sailing" for you and you're "on course" in your waking life. Obviously, the opposite is true if the conditions are rough with crashing, high waves. Since water represents the emotions, it could be highlighting your relationships, either at home or with your friends. In the dream, if a storm is brewing, or perhaps it's raging, it's describing challenges ahead. If the boat sinks, perhaps a hope has been dashed, an idea has sunk without trace or you may have to ditch a current plan. Are you drifting with the tide and going nowhere or just "going with the flow" in your real life? Watching a boat sail away from the shore indicates a lost opportunity you may regret.

Boyfriends

For girls, this could be a predictive dream, so if you don't have a boyfriend at the moment and have been living in

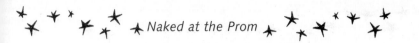
hope, keep your eyes open – you could be meeting some-one soon! Kissing a boyfriend in a dream suggests you need to be loved. If your boyfriend is kissing someone else in your dream, it's likely you've already had suspicions about his loyalty to you in real life. If so, this dream may be giving you some clues about him. Or perhaps you suffer from jealousy and the dream is presenting an opportunity to work things out for yourself before you spoil something good. People can appear differently in dreams yet you know who they are. For example, in your dream, your real-life boyfriend may have the face of your brother or even someone famous. Your subconscious is pointing out how similar someone in real life is to the person in the dream. They have common characteristics or looks that you really like.

Candles

Candles are symbols of wisdom and understanding. When lit, they show illumination, either a light in the darkness sig-nifying hope and improvement, or perhaps a brilliant idea that is about to come into your head. The glow of a candle is a good omen for contentment and strong relationships. Should the candle go out, a disappointment may be in store. If it flickers, get set for new opportunities and a total

change. Because of its shape, a candle can also be a phallic symbol, and may suggest you're feeling sexy.

Cars/Driving

In whatever way a car appears in a dream, it represents your energy, your "drive," the way you are "driven" to do things. If something goes wrong with the car in the dream – if, for instance, you're driving along and the brakes fail and you lose control of the vehicle – this could be an indication that you're not using your talents properly. This particular dream may be referring to a real-life situation where you're "out of control" and need to put the brakes on before things run away with you! Such a dream can also be predictive, a warning that your car in real life needs to have the brakes checked. Running out of gas can suggest that you're physically low in energy, or running on empty. If the clutch in your dream car won't work it shows your energy is being misdirected. Essentially, you can't get yourself into the right gear; perhaps you've lost your hold on a matter or you're wasting your time. If you have to push the car, it means either that you're pushing yourself with great effort or you need a bit of a shove to get yourself moving. You'll know which applies to you because in real life you'll either be working hard or a bit on the lazy side. A crash can indicate things are totally out of control in your life, or is a warning that they're heading that way fast. Do note the road conditions in the dream – whether you're on a rough road or a clear highway – because this is describing how

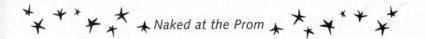

your present pathway is looking! The size, make, color and condition of a car are also important in the dream. These details give many clues, and of course the condition of the car speaks for itself. If it's rusty, this says you have let things slip and it's time you did something to improve your image and style; if it's shiny, you are sparkling and in good condition to travel into the next phase of life's journey. The color of the car may be better understood in dream lore by reading the entry on Colors.

Castles

It's a good omen to dream of a beautiful castle. Riches and opportunities are manifest in this symbol. Because of their fortress-like construction, dream castles can be a sign of security – up goes the drawbridge, for example, and you are safe inside. If the castle is in ruins then your plans will come to nothing. If clouds surround the spires or towers, ask yourself if you're just building castles in the air with unrealistic ideas or plans.

Cats

In dreams, cats represent intuitions and instincts. In waking life, how do you feel about them? Do you like them, loathe them or not really care? A cat is generally a good animal to appear in a dream, conveying help, quiet strength and guidance.

Long ago in Egypt, cats were revered and in the temples acted as guardians, so you need to examine the context of your dream closely to see how the cat presents itself. It could be your guardian appearing to you and asking you to pay more attention to your intuition. What did your cat show you or teach you in the dream? A person can behave in a "catty" way, and if the cat you saw was aggressive, who was it representing in real life? Does the cat in your dream remind you of someone you know? Or could it even be you? We talk about the "lucky black cat" so its color may also be an important clue in your dream.

Cemeteries – see Graveyards

Classrooms

Dreaming of a classroom is telling you that you are about to learn or discover something that will help you make better progress in the waking world. Is there something written on the black- or whiteboard in the dream? If so, is it a cryptic message that you need to think about and decode? Is the atmosphere calm or unruly? Perhaps there has been an incident in the classroom that needs to be unraveled. Are you in conflict with the teacher and are you listening to what is being said? Finally, is there a predominant color in the clothing people are wearing? If so, see Colors for more

information. In dream lore, the classroom symbolizes a part of ourselves and the action there describes and reflects what is happening to us and what we are feeling. It's important, then, to identify this with your waking life because it could also be a warning of some kind.

Climbing

A dream about climbing symbolizes ambition and a desire to succeed. The measure of your success is shown by the ease with which you are doing the climbing. The harder the climb and the more difficulties you are having to overcome in your dream, the harder it is to reach your goal in real life. If you're going up a staircase, are the steps firm or rickety? If you're climbing a mountain, is the track you're following smooth or stony? If you're going up a ladder, is it shiny and modern or old, unstable and with missing rungs? You really need to take everything into consideration to interpret this dream correctly. If you eventually reach the top after a hard climb you know that, despite obstacles, your hard work and determination will pay off. An easy climb shows that you'll find it a cinch to achieve your aims, but where did the climb lead you? Moving down steps or stairs may indicate problems or setbacks, but it could also mean that you have some unfinished business to attend to. In this case, your Dream Self is telling you that you need to gather more facts, or that the information you need is stored deeper down in your memory.

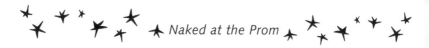

Clothes

Dreams about clothes and other trendy things are all about self-image. Dreaming of wearing something old or ridiculous, or possessing objects that are unfashionable and make you feel embarrassed, indicates a lack of self-confidence and suggests you're worrying too much about what others think of you. This could be your subconscious subtly pointing out what kind of values you are placing on yourself. Check the colors of items in the dream to reveal more about your image. Dark shades suggest an attempt to conceal your image, while bright colorful things suggest you want to be noticed. Your dream might even inspire you to start a new fashion trend.

College – see University

Colors

Colors have their own special, descriptive language in dreams. We don't always dream in color and some people swear they dream only in black and white. Research suggests the messages conveyed are equally important in both types of dream. A dream in black and white might be suggesting that you're seeing a situation as too clear-cut, all "black and white" with no gray areas. During much of your dream time you probably won't even notice whether the dream's in color or not, but sometimes a really bright color

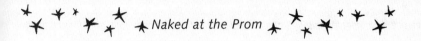

will strike you and stay in your mind. The significance of that color then becomes a key part of your interpretation.

Black

Black is considered negative and therefore suggests doom and gloom or something happening that is underhanded, hidden or even mysterious. When in waking life we say "things are looking black," we mean there doesn't seem to be any way forward, and so the blackness or bleakness is despair, perhaps grieving for something that we've lost. The color black signifies a moving pause, a transition that we must move through until the new light appears, like the night gradually leading to a new dawn. Black can actually be restful.

Blue

Clear blue has depth, calm and peace. It makes you think of blue skies and clear, blue water. This color is associated with loyalty, truth and justice as well as with cooperation and teamwork. Wherever it appears in the dream, it is commu- nicating these qualities to you with hope and clarity and encouraging harmony in all your affairs. A darker, muddier or moodier version of blue conveys depression, or a fit of "the blues." Perhaps in show- ing you this murkier shade, your subconscious is

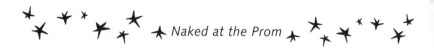

telling you either to avoid something or to find a more positive route!

Gold

The sun is associated with gold and there is a splendor about it. In dreams, gold symbolizes success and achievement – and often riches and wealth, too. In the subtle language of dreams, seeing this color indicates you have reached a very rewarding phase in your life.

Green

Because green is the color of nature, we see it all around us in waking life. Green is for healing, nurturing and soothing, so if it's dominant in your dream scene, you are balancing and healing all your energies while your physical body rests. This color conveys hope and opportunity to start something new. When green is dull or dark, it's showing decline and decay or a lack of strength and vitality. Perhaps it means you need more sleep, a better diet, or a boost of vitamins. "Green as grass," the expression used for being naive or immature, can crop up in a dream scene. For example, you might be playing games on the lawn and get covered in bits of grass or grass stains. Here your subconscious is inferring that you need to grow up and take more responsibility for yourself!

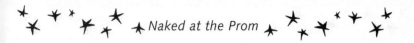

Orange

Orange is a refreshing, bright and zingy color that you just can't miss. It always seems to say, "I'm here!" This color brings happiness and cheer and is the rejuvenating color, so if it appears in your dream that is its message. It means that something will happen to lift and balance your feelings and give you pizzazz. If someone is wearing orange in the dream, they are seeking attention. Orange is the color of confidence, telling you to believe in yourself and to go for it!

Pink

To dream of shades of rose, pink or peach means peace and happiness. Sayings like "being in the pink" (meaning happy and healthy) or "everything is just peachy" reflect a state of loving warmth and contentment in your dream. There is a simplicity in this color and the message it conveys to you in your sleep is a beautiful and loving one.

Red

Red symbolizes either passionate love or raging anger. Red roses are sent on special occasions as a loving gesture, and if they appear in a dream they are conveying special love to you. The expression "red flag to a bull" means a taunting and teasing

situation that leads to rage and anger, and this
may be describing what's going on in your life at
the moment. Check out who the angry one is in
the dream; it may be you or perhaps you're the
one who's aggravating others with your attitude
or behavior. Red also denotes vitality and energy
and is associated with the heart, blood circulation
and spine. The dream could be connecting you to
a health matter, so check the context. But red is
also a festive color indicating celebration, so
perhaps you'll soon be "painting the town red."

Silver

If you dream of silver as a precious metal, perhaps
as a piece of jewelry, it means that an idea, pure
and simple, is about to come to you. Silver is a
feminine symbol and it is associated with the
moon and moonlight. But moonlight makes things
shimmery, so this dream could be telling you that
a plan you're developing is not yet clear and needs
working on. If there's a lot of silver in your dream,
your subconscious is telling you to use your
intuition more. If you're wearing silvery clothes,

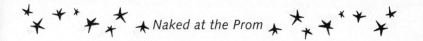

your Dream Self may be suggesting you're too romantic or idealistic. Perhaps it's time to see things more realistically.

Violet

Shades of purple from violet through lavender to lilac are the colors of the 21st century. They are known primarily as "spiritual" colors and when they appear in dreams they are conveying intelligence, knowledge, devotion and dignity. Violet is a color of sensitivity and high ideals, so take its message to heart. Perhaps it means you're being oversensitive or, alternatively, perhaps not sensitive enough. Generally, this is a wonderful color to see in a dream because it has transforming qualities and puts everything into true perspective.

White

White indicates a fresh start, something totally new and inspirational. It symbolizes purity and protection in any context. Perhaps you saw a shaft of light coming into your dream. This suggests that something is being highlighted or illuminated and it means you will receive the go-ahead for a project or have a brilliant idea. After all, when we have a revelation we say that we are "seeing the light." Or was the white object in your dream a clean sheet of paper ready for you to write on?

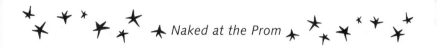

If so, this could indicate the beginning of a new chapter in your life.

Yellow

When you see yellow in your dream as a vibrant, clear color, it symbolizes intellect, creativity and intuition. Its message is to enhance and promote your thoughts, ideas and artistic abilities. Just as the sun, daffodils and buttercups radiate golden yellow warmth in nature, so light and laughter will be coming into your life soon. If you see a greenish yellow then beware: envy or jealousy is connected with this shade. Or might your yellow dream be a message about cowardice, since we do associate this color with spineless behavior? Beware, too, if you dream of a wishy-washy yellow – your subconscious may be telling you that you're low in energy and need rest or even a trip to the doctor.

Computers

To dream of a computer, or working at one, suggests you need to apply logic to a situation. You are really going to have to work something out very soon, or even sooner! Are you playing a computer game in the dream or writing a pro-gram, or are you in "search" mode trying to find some information? The image of the computer is suggesting that you can improve yourself and increase your knowledge with

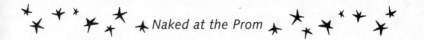

application and coordination; that is, by bringing a number of your skills together.

Crocodiles

How do you view crocodiles and alligators in waking life? You may be one of the few who aren't bothered by them. Generally, however, it is not good news to dream of these creatures because their image is tied to a warning. These reptiles are associated with hypocrisy and lies, illustrated by the phrase "to shed crocodile tears," meaning pretending to be sorry when the reverse is the case. An open mouth full of teeth is a bit scary, and the snapping action of the jaws could give you a clue as to what the dream is about. Perhaps you or someone you know has been rather snappy lately. Crocodiles live on both land and water, which means they have a dual nature. They also hide themselves well. Take care in your life right now – there are hidden factors, even treachery, that could catch you unawares.

Crying

Crying in dreams is about releasing emotional stress, so although it isn't pleasant, it's a very healthy experience. In waking life, it's likely you will have recently been upset, but the dream could be referring to an incident that happened a long time ago. Dream crying is a way for your subconscious to deal with some unfinished grieving or sense of loss.

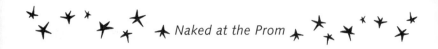

Daggers

Daggers, swords and spears have a very strong connection in symbolism. They are masculine, showing power, authority, determination, courage and justice. But they can show anger, or a lust for justice. So, with these many different meanings, the context of your dream and the circumstances in your waking life are the key factors in unraveling the message. Remember, anything you hold, like a dagger, for instance, is really an extension of yourself that needs to wield power. The dagger gives emphasis to the part you are playing in the dream. Is it being used by you or someone else; and is it for attack or defense? Basically, are you the hunter or the hunted in your dream? Is your Dream Self warning you of someone in real life who is likely to "stab you in the back," or could that possibly be you on the attack, determined to get someone? Sometimes, just the image may show up, perhaps floating in front of you, or the dagger may be handed to you. In this case you are being handed authority and the power to go forward. The meaning of the dagger will depend on how you feel when you are having the dream. If you are anxious or afraid then perhaps in real life you're feeling threatened by something or

someone. And since a dagger is also a phallic symbol, this fear may be connected with anxiety about sex.

Death

Many people get upset by dreams of death, but usually they simply indicate a major change, a transition from the old to the new. It's extremely rare that a dream of this sort means someone is going to die, although it can sometimes be a disturbing dream to experience. The message is about the opportunity to transform and release fears and phobias held from the past. Endings and beginnings are very tightly woven together – you can't have one without the other. This kind of dream is part of your natural processing where you are unloading unnecessary baggage in order to move on to better things. So, rather than a negative dream, this one has a very positive message.

Diamonds

These glorious stones carry the symbolism of truth and beauty. It's a good image to dream about, especially if the stones are brilliant! If you are being given a diamond then good fortune, perhaps money, is coming your way. If you lose a diamond in the dream it suggests you may be fearful of losing something you consider precious. A cut diamond has many facets, so if it appears in front of you, perhaps twinkling and shining and turning, it is symbolizing that you need to look at all the different aspects of a situation. It is

saying you should consider the bigger picture before jumping to conclusions.

Dieting

If you dream that you're on a diet, it could simply be that food or losing weight has been on your mind, or perhaps you've been reading about the latest diet fad. But since dieting is to do with "reducing," this could be a signal to cut down on any type of excess in your waking life. It's a nudge prompting you to find ways and means to trim, save, become less extravagant. This dream is also telling you that you shouldn't become diverted by unnecessary activities at this time in your life.

Dogs

Loyalty, friendship and guardianship are the key words when a dog appears in your dream. Generally, dogs are thought of as messengers. But if you are afraid of them in waking life, seeing a dog will act as a warning. A dog bite may be telling you to be wary of someone you thought was a good friend. As with all dreams, the context will point to who, where or what you should be careful of. Thinking about the characteristics we associate with dogs will help you work out your dream. For example, guard dogs imply protection; dogs can "sniff things out," or you could be "barking up the wrong tree." Does the dog in the dream remind you of someone? If so, what is it doing and what

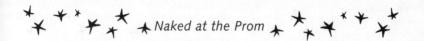
does this tell you about that person in real life? Always note the breed of dog when you recall your dream since this, too, may provide clues. For example, a St. Bernard is a rescue dog, while sheep dogs are for gathering and collecting. If you're walking with a guide dog the message may be that you are blind to a certain situation in waking life. The advice is clear – take another look.

Dolphins

These wonderful creatures have taken on new symbolism for the 21st century, so to dream of dolphins is great – your Dream Self is keeping you up to date! In real life, these are creatures who will play with us and they are now known to convey healing and a sense of well-being. In the dream world they come as teachers, using play and their unique sound – just as they do in real life. When dolphins appear in a dream you

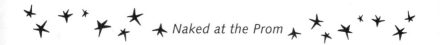

are being shown how to lighten up on some of your attitudes and how to use your intuition to better advantage. In ancient times, dolphins were greatly revered, especially by sailors who recognized them as guardians of the ocean, helping to guide their ships through storms. Guardianship and guiding through troubled waters (and remember that water in our dreams represents our emotions) are always a part of the meaning whenever you dream about a dolphin.

Doors

The door symbol has many beautiful meanings. An open door, for example, is an opportunity. You're ready to go through or to enter the next phase of development in your life. Note the shape and color of the door because these can give you valuable clues to what is going on in your life. A closed door may be saying that the time isn't right for you to move to the next stage. If you knock, turn the key or the door handle in an attempt to find what is on the other side, it means you can bring your plans to fruition with a little more effort. If you are being chased down an alley and end up at a closed door, take the warning that you're "going down a blind alley" in your waking life.

Doves

Known internationally as the symbol of peace, a dove can bring hope, communication, love and calm when it appears

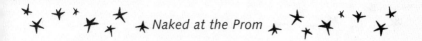

in your dream. Perhaps this is what you need in your life right now, or maybe more specifically the dream is saying you need to bring peace into your life. Perhaps you are being shown encouragement to become the "peacemaker" in a situation in waking life. Whatever the case, this dream brings a very positive, personal message.

Driving – see Cars/Driving

Drowning

This dream is usually a bit of a nightmare. Suffocating is another version of the same type of dream. It is certainly a releasing act by your Dream Self, so in this respect drowning in your dream can have a beneficial side to it – although it may not feel like it at the time! The water element is so powerful that when you experience it like this you know you will either sink or swim. And that is the situation your dream is describing about in your real life. Water, as we know, refers to our emotions so perhaps if you're drowning, it means you're being swamped or overwhelmed by your feelings. Perhaps you're going through a relationship problem of some kind. Perhaps you feel you're in too deep and you're uncomfortable about it. If you're sinking into mud in your dream, it can mean you're overburdened with responsibilities or swamped by exams or other work. Whatever the situation, the dream is suggesting you need to "come up for air."

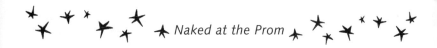

* & *

Eagles

An eagle symbolizes power, creation, exploration and clear sight. Dreaming of this majestic bird represents an opportunity to soar above the rest and move ahead with your ambitions and vision. Like the eagle circling above, you need to employ patience and wait for the right moment to make your move, but the power to realize your plans is already in your life because the eagle brings this gift through your dream. An eagle dream may also be bidding you to use your "eagle eye" in your waking life, especially if you're involved in any creative projects.

Eating

A dream in which you're eating can have several different meanings. Perhaps in real life you're "chewing over matters" or going through a boring patch and need the "taste" of a new experience. Could it be that you're overreacting and "making a meal" of a certain situation in real life? Perhaps you have something important to think about – in other words, "food for thought." Eating is generally considered a social event, so this dream may be asking you to

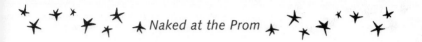

be more cooperative or to share more in family activity. A banquet foretells a big celebration.

Embarrassment

Embarrassment dreams are really quite common and we all, at some time or other, dream about things that make us cringe. In general, we have this type of dream when we're feeling vulnerable or lacking in self-confidence. For example, a dream where you're walking naked down the street is connected with anxiety, or a secret worry, about being ridiculed in waking life. A dream where you are trying to find a toilet is a physical response and often just a nudge to wake up and go to the bathroom! You may also find yourself in a dream wearing the wrong clothes at a fancy event, and again this shows you are perhaps suffering with shyness and afraid of showing yourself in public. Or perhaps it indicates that you're feeling a bit of an outcast because all your friends are getting some new clothes and you aren't able to keep up with the in-crowd or with the latest fashion. (See also Nudity and Bathrooms.)

Escaping

This is another fairly common type of dream. Basically, it's all about taking responsibility and the desire to gain freedom. Of course, very often you're under pressure in this dream, frightened and in a panic. What are you escaping from in your dream, and where do you end up? As with all dreams,

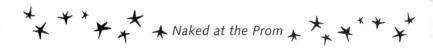

this one is telling you something about your real life – in this case your desire to get in control of or to release yourself from a particular situation. Perhaps you need to face up to a decision. It could simply mean that you have lots of excess energy and need to let off steam. Perhaps you need to be more physical, so get active and exercise.

Exams

If you're taking a test and you can't answer any of the questions or, alternatively, the test paper is blank, or you forgot to bring your pencil, these are all classic examples of anxieties in waking life surfacing in dreams. You may have a terrific fear of failure programmed into your mind or you're being tested by someone in waking life. Perhaps you have neglected homework or missed out on lessons or lectures. On the positive side, some people actually dream of the questions that are coming up in a test – so do try to read and remember any test paper that appears in a dream. It could prove very helpful!

Eyes

Strange as it may sound, it's quite common to see the image of an eye floating towards you in dreams – it's "eye-catching"! Actually, the message here is that you need to focus your attention on something. Perhaps this dream is telling you that you need to be more watchful. On a

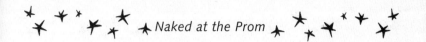
different level, if instead of "eye" you read "I" – your sub-conscious likes to keep you on your toes by playing these funny word games – it could mean that your hidden individuality is calling out for attention. Maybe you need to be more center-stage, more visible among your peers. Looking into a pair of eyes is similar to looking into a mirror. After all, the eyes are said to be the "mirrors of the soul," and this is a deep, emotional and personal experience. Love and compassion may be reflected back to you at a time when you need it. Blue eyes are for peace and healing and brown eyes are for comfort and practical support. Any kind of defect or injury to the eyes or vision highlights a lack of clarity and focus in your real life. Your Dream Self may be telling you that you're just not "seeing" the obvious.

Falling

This common dream often indicates a lack of confidence, a sense of insecurity or fear of failure. It's probably reflecting a situation in your life that's making you feel anxious: taking a test, for example. Perhaps you have a certain reputation to keep up and you're afraid if you relax your guard you'll lose ground. Falling in a dream can also be connected to a fear of heights in real life.

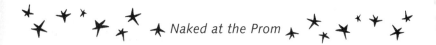

Fame

Dreaming of fame is about seeking attention; it also is linked to the word "fortune." Being famous in a dream is simply processing your fantasies that are being played out for you as you sleep. This dream also spurs you on to work harder in order to realize your full potential. If you meet a celebrity in your dream or are surrounded by famous people, you could be needing more recognition in the real world.

Family

Dreams about your family reflect something about your relationships and attitudes to family life – perhaps an issue to do with loyalty or unity. The dream may be triggered by something that recently happened at home. Through the feelings and behavior in your dream, you may see a family member in a different light, or gain a new understanding about your own role in the family. In dream lore, a happy family gathering is an indication that good fortune and contentment are on the way.

Father figures

How does this father image appear in your dream, and is it your own father or someone else's? How you get on with your father in waking life affects how you understand what the dream is releasing and reflecting. When your father appears as himself, it may be a reflection of an event that happened in the day. Sometimes in dreams fathers, princi-

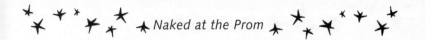

pals or policemen are all interchangeable because in the symbology of dreams they represent authority and power. Perhaps it means you need to seek advice, or stick to the rules. Beware if the father figure is antagonistic towards you – it could mean you're in for a scolding! A reassuring dream is to see a father in a happy, carefree mood, since it means approval and indicates that things in real life are going well.

Fences

If in a dream you're stopped by a fence or a barrier then you're probably feeling "fenced in" at the moment. Are you being stopped from doing something you want to do in waking life, or have you deliberately put up the fence yourself? Look at what is behind the fence. Is it a beautiful place? If so, it means everything is great in your life within the boundaries you have set yourself. But if it is rough, horrible or miserable, it reflects your present anxieties and worries. Look over the fence. If what you see is better on the other side, your subconscious is showing you that things can improve if you make the effort and find a way of overcoming the barrier. (See also Walls.)

Fighting

Fighting in a dream means you have some kind of conflict going on in waking life. Should you wake up still fighting, you are struggling with anger or frustration that you can't overcome. It's much better news if you win the fight against

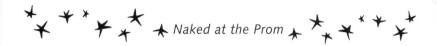

your aggressor, because this means you will find a solution to the problem. This dream can also be a warning that you may need to stick up for yourself.

Fire

Dreams about fire represent your energy levels and enthusiasm for life. You're probably being challenged in waking life to put a lot of your energy into an activity or project. A warm, cozy fireplace is a good image spelling contentment and security. To dream about a burning building suggests that your inner emotions are getting out of control. Lighting a fire is a signal to get started on a project or plan. A fire that suddenly flares up is like anger and a warning sign that perhaps you'd better "cool it." If you're in love, dreams of fire could be describing the passion of your feelings.

Flowers – see Gardens

Flying

Flying in dreams is very common. If you're flying high it indicates ambition. Soaring like an eagle is a powerful omen – keeping an eye open for an opportunity. Flying into clouds suggests you could be moving into a no-go or foggy situation. Or perhaps it means you aren't being realistic and have your "head in the clouds"! If you're dream-flying at night and seeing the stars above and the land below makes you feel happy and contented, it means you've reached a point

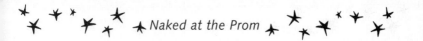

in your real life where you're secure and confident to explore whatever adventures life has in store.

Friends

When dreaming of friends, what they say and do is key to the meaning of your dream. This will show you how in real life you see your place in the group. Basically, it's about your current situation, both at home and outside. A dream where you fight with your best friend may be foretelling that you're about to break up. Differences of opinion show that you've felt either let down by or disappointed with some-one you know. You may have been angry (see Fighting) and expressed your desire to sort out the situation. Good friends are supportive and affectionate and to experience a happy dream in their company is obviously a sign that things are currently going well in your life.

Gardens

Gardens are normally associated with peace, beauty and fra-grance, so dreaming of one foretells contentment and harmony. However, if your dream garden is overgrown, messy or run down, something in your waking life needs a bit of care, attention and clearing up. Perhaps this is pointing

to your bad habits, taking too much for granted, or care-lessness. When the flowers or bushes in the dream garden are wilting or dying, it shows your talents are going to waste and more concentration on your work is required. If you are walking down a garden path in the dream, note its condition and where it leads you. If it's all stony and neg-lected, you may be going through problems. But if it's pretty and pleasant, things are going well in your life.

Donna's dream

Donna was going through a difficult time. Her parents had been arguing for years and finally decided to get divorced. Glad that the yelling and bad feelings were going to stop, she was still upset about the break-up of the family and the inevitable changes that lay ahead. The night her mother broke the news to her about the divorce, Donna had a dream. She dreamed she was walking along a rocky path, with nettles stinging her legs. She was very sad and sat on a large rock and cried. Eventually she dried her tears and then, looking into the distance, she saw a beautiful garden filled with lovely flowers and lush trees. People were walking in the garden, pointing to the blossoms, laughing and playing games. Suddenly she felt happier than she'd been for months and woke up with a good feeling of calm and peace.

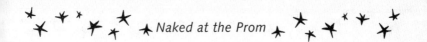

Our dreams are often messages, showing us what lies in store. In Donna's dream, her subconscious is describing her life like the road on which she finds herself – difficult, rocky and full of pain.

But the dream goes on to show her what the future holds, that despite her sadness now there are happier times ahead. Gardens are always signs of contentment and hope, and the happy people in Donna's dream confirm that after the divorce things will work out for the best and everyone concerned will be much happier than they are now.

Ghosts

We are more likely to dream about ghosts after watching a spooky movie. It's just your Dream Self clearing away these frightening thoughts and images. In our waking lives, lots of unpleasant, negative things happen to us, such as people picking fights or saying abusive things. A ghostly presence in your dream might be representing this experience or person, bringing out the fear rather than letting it get buried in your subconscious where it can do damage. If in the dream your reaction to the ghost is calm, your Dream Self is showing that you can cope with the unexpected or deal with whatever lies ahead.

Girlfriends

For boys, this kind of dream can be the result of wishful thinking, especially if you don't have a special girlfriend. It can also be a predictive type of dream, showing that you are going to meet a new girlfriend soon. Jealousy often plays itself out by dreaming your girlfriend is with someone else. Recall as many clues as you can so as to make sense of the dream's message. Colors, clothes and the surroundings all hold valuable clues. How you feel in the dream is most important. This can help you to discover how your girlfriend feels about you in your waking life, and it may also help you to sort out some of your fantasies.

Graveyards

Dreaming of being in a graveyard is often the result of watching a scary movie before bed. Nevertheless, this is still a valuable dream so note what happens and what you see. Very often a name on a tombstone is prominent, but it won't have anything to do with death or someone dying – it's just a means for your subconscious to communicate information. It's written for you on the headstone because it's "grave" or serious enough to remind you to do some-thing. Perhaps the cemetery scene is a reflection of your loneliness or a feeling of isolation in waking life. If in your dream you are present at a burial, the message is about the pressures of life, work overload or a desire to "bury" the past or to end a real-life relationship.

Guns

Gunfire in a dream acts as a warning of something that's going to happen in waking life. Think of a starting gun that is fired to set off a race. Transfer this idea to your present real life. It may reflect how you're feeling about your part in a situation – nervous but wanting to win. Being shot at in a dream can indicate you have an enemy, and if a gun is just being pointed at you, the message is about feeling threatened. But who is holding the gun? Guns are also a phallic symbol, so a sexual matter could be a hidden factor in this dream.

Hair

Dreaming of hair is drawing your attention to how you're feeling about yourself right now. It's all about your self-esteem and your state of health. To dream of glossy, thick hair indicates good health, but hair loss or dry, sparse hair is a warning that your self-esteem is low and you need some tender loving care. Combing hair and sorting out the tangles shows your ability to solve a current problem. Braiding hair indicates a new friendship. Having your hair cut reveals a new start, a new image. Washing your hair or standing under a waterfall or shower is all about cleansing – washing out the old so you can emerge fresh and sparkling from head to toe. (See also Washing.)

Hands

Your sensitivity is being highlighted when you dream of hands. Injuries, such as losing fingers, indicate a guilt complex. Burned fingers or hands show a fear of making mistakes and being unable to make the right decisions. If you see one hand with the palm held up towards you, it's a sign to "stop." Using your hands in a clumsy way may mean you're unable to "hold on" to a situation in real life, you may be "losing your touch" or finding things "hard to handle." If you are reaching out and can't get to something, this could mean you are "out of touch" and have neglected work, friends or yourself.

Horses

Horses are symbols of strength and wisdom, and they represent the swiftness of thought and the speed of light. Sitting astride a horse hints at a rise in fortune, while falling off indicates your future plans will take a tumble. Seeing a galloping stallion implies imminent success. Riding a horse is a comment on your progress in real life. If the horse is galloping out of control and you're holding on for dear life, it could mean you're struggling with certain subjects in school. A gentle trot, on the other hand, shows that life is okay.

Hospitals

Buildings in dreams can represent ourselves, and since hospitals are places of healing we tend to dream of them when

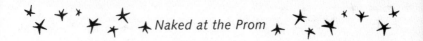

we're run down or feeling ill. This dream therefore is a message that you need to take better care of yourself and your health. It can also be a useful reminder that you need to keep a doctor's appointment.

Houses

A dream about a house is connected with your body and yourself. The different floors and rooms all represent a separate aspect of your personality and your life. If you dream about a basement or cellar, you are connecting to the deep, hidden area of your character where talents, fears and memories lie buried. If you go up the stairs, it means your fortunes are on the rise – you're going up in the world! The top of the house represents your hopes and ambitions. The condition of the house describes what is going on in your life. A chaotic mess denotes confused and cluttered ideas, or complications with your relationships. Bright, clean and tidy rooms indicate that you're on top of things and all is progressing well. Entering an empty room during a dream may be an indication of loneliness or an emptiness in your waking life. Perhaps it means it's time to make new friends or take up new hobbies to fill the void. The condition of the outside of the house in the dream also gives you important information, this time about your image. Perhaps you need a make-over and some sprucing up, a new hairstyle or more fashionable clothes. (See also Windows.)

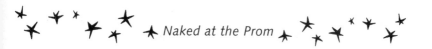

Sally's dream

Sally's relationship with her new boyfriend inten-
sified soon after they met. After a seriously heavy
make-out session she had a dream that she was in
a strange house. Not knowing her way around the
building, she found herself opening a door that led
down to a basement. The area below was dark,
but she was curious to explore this part of the
house and began climbing down the steps to the
room below.

In our dreams, houses represent our bodies, and
basement areas are the secret or hidden aspects of
our lives that are yet to be discovered. Often, the
basement symbolizes our sexual curiosity, so Sally's
dream was a reflection of her feelings at that time.

Illness

Dreaming that you're ill can sometimes be an advance
warning because one of the jobs of the subconscious is to
maintain and repair the physical body. If you're a bit off in

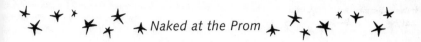

waking life, the dream may be advising you to take action, such as going to the doctor. When you wake up try to remember any detail in the dream that locates and identifies the illness. If you dream that someone, or even a pet, is ill, it could mean that you're worried about them. On a different level of meaning altogether, the dream may be telling you that your current plans aren't "healthy," so think again.

Insects

Generally, insects are thought of as unpleasant, even hostile in nature, so dreaming about them infers you are being irritated or annoyed by petty issues in your life. Swarms of bees, wasps or ants show that you're anxious about certain details in your work or life. Butterflies, though, are very fortunate and indicate success and a transformation in your life. Dark moths suggest that someone or something is "bugging" you and you will need to take some positive action in order to get your plans off the ground.

Invisibility

To dream that you are invisible indicates a desire to disappear and perhaps leave something or someone behind. It represents an escape from responsibilities, embarrassment or difficulties when you can see no other way out. Shyness is often part of this dream, as is thinking you're too fat, too thin or even worthless. If people disappear in front of you in the dream, the message is the same – a feeling of insignifi-

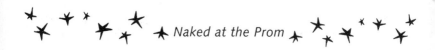
cance is being reflected and it's time to become more expressive in waking life, develop your talents, join in more and make yourself more prominent!

Islands

Being on an island in a dream hints at feelings of isolation in waking life – you either want to get away from it all or you want to be rescued. Water surrounding the island represents the emotional challenges in your daily life. The island represents safe ground for the time being, so in this respect it's a good omen. But it's not so good if your waking life is on hold, because the island mentality reflects your present loneliness.

Jewels/jewelry

To dream of bright, shining jewels is a good omen indicating good fortune, especially for your ambitions. But if they are dull, broken or the settings tarnished, there are disappointments ahead. If you lose jewels or jewelry in a dream, take heed – this warns of problems ahead, possibly involving money. If you find an item of jewelry in your dream, you can expect something really good to turn up soon. On a higher level of understanding, jewels symbolize the hidden treasures of truth and knowledge, so they may be an indi-

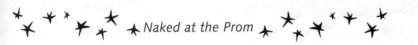
cation that you'll learn something important soon. (See also Diamonds.)

Journeys

A dream journey of any kind – on foot, by car, train, bike or plane – symbolizes your journey through life. In the dream, if you're at the beginning of the journey or setting off, it marks the start of a new phase, a new adventure in waking life. If you're just traveling along and enjoying everything around you, you're at a contented, easy stage when things bode well in your life. Difficulties on the road or bleak surroundings reflect your present problems in life. For example, climbing over boulders shows obstacles, whereas a stroll means things are going well. There are countless clues to consider in the landscape, and the people you meet and the colors you see all contain hidden messages for you to decipher when you wake up.

Jugglers

Either seeing or being a juggler in a dream reflects your abilities, dexterity and skills in life just now. If you can keep all the balls in the air, it means you're amazing and coping well with all the pressures you're under in your waking life. When you miss catches and things are falling around you, it's a warning that things are getting "out of hand."

Take time out to regroup or drop out of some of the less important activities you're currently involved in.

Keys

A key is a delightful symbol to see in your dream because it allows you to open up to new possibilities. Dreaming that you find a key foretells that you are about to find a solution to something in waking life. To lose a key is a warning that you may miss an opportunity or fail at something. If someone in the dream hands you a key it could mean you're getting serious about someone because you're receiving the "key to their heart." (See also Prisons.)

Killing

Dreams of killing can be triggered by watching a violent movie before bed. However, to dream about killing something or someone usually means you're coming to the end of a project, a phase, a relationship or a stage of your life and are about to begin something new. If you were doing the killing, your Dream Self may simply be processing the anger you were feeling during the day. Or it could be telling you that it's time to stop something, or that now is the right time to end a friendship.

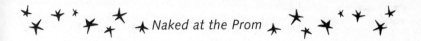

Kings

Dreaming of royalty often indicates that you have a need to be noticed. It also denotes power – being "monarch of all you see" – and so it's showing that you're aspiring to regal qualities. If you see a crown or, better still, if you're being crowned, it means that success and rewards are coming to you in real life. Sometimes, a dream king will refer to someone you know whose last name is King and so your dream will involve that person.

Kissing

Kissing often occurs in wish-fulfillment dreams, but generally it's symbolic of a loving and affectionate situation. A kiss from a family member in a dream represents the strength of your bond with them. To be kissed in a dream shows approval. But to be kissed by someone you don't like reflects distaste and could be a warning that you may soon face a task you don't like in waking life. Also, heed the warning about "kiss and tell," especially if there was a lot of whispering going on in your dream. It could mean one of your friends is deceiving and/or two-timing you.

Kitchens

This room is considered to be the center of the home, and the house itself symbolizes you and your personality. So the kitchen in your dream is reflecting something that is close to

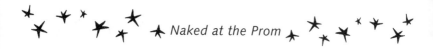

your heart – your family, perhaps. Try to remember the conditions in the kitchen. If it is clean and tidy, it means things are going well for you in real life. If the room is a mess, it could be an indication that you're confused about something, or that you've had an argument with your parents. If you're happily cooking in the dream it means you're being creative and are currently developing some good ideas and plans in your waking life.

Knots

To dream about a knot refers to an entanglement or a complex situation in your real life. If you untie a knot, it shows that you will sort things out. If you're tying string into a big ball, your subconscious may be telling you that you're making a simple situation unnecessarily complicated. Are you tying up loose ends in your dream? If so, you need to finish off all those unfinished projects you've got lying around.

Ladders

A ladder is an important dream symbol because it relates to hopes and ambitions and your ability to move into something new. "Successfully climbing the ladder" and "one

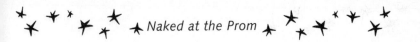
more rung up the ladder" refer to "going up in the world." If in your dream you are climbing up a ladder with no problems, you are moving into a successful period. If you find it difficult – perhaps there were missing rungs or you are nervous or frightened about going any further – your subconscious is reflecting your anxieties and lack of confidence in your waking life. Reaching the top shows you're about to achieve a long-held ambition.

Legs

Dreaming that your legs are as heavy as lead and you just can't run is fairly common. It's warning you of difficulties in your real life or telling you that you have to do something you'd rather not do: take an important test, for example. To hurt your legs or knees in a dream is a warning that you need to slow down and not be so impulsive in your waking life.

Letters

Letters represent communication and receiving one in your dream means news is on its way in real life. Try to remember what the letter says since this will give you clues as to what you can soon expect to hear.

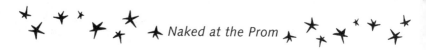
Libraries

In the waking world libraries store knowledge, so this dream will have something to do with learning and discovering things. Dreaming that you're in a library may be a prompt from your subconscious urging you to remember something important. Perhaps it's telling you to search for an aspect of yourself that has been buried back in your past when you were little. If you're searching for a book, the title or the story will give you a clue to the meaning of the dream. Alternatively, this may simply be a reminder that it's time to renew your library books.

Lights

A dream where light appears refers to something being illuminated or cleared up for you, especially if you've been confused in your waking life. If you see a light-bulb, expect an answer or solution to a problem to come to you shortly. The color of the bulb may give you a clue about what's going on in your real life. Red could be a warning to stop something, whereas green gives permission to proceed. If you see light flooding through an open door this is a sign that something new is opening up for you. Lots of people dream of seeing a light at the end of a tunnel, which means that things in real life are getting better. (See also Tunnels.)

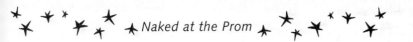
Lions

Whether in real life or in dreams, lions represent strength and courage. If you're the lion, it means that you are, or can be, strong. But lions can also be scary creatures and to be chased by one in your dream means that someone or something in your waking life is making you anxious. This is something that you need to sort out. Talking or playing with a lion shows that you can deal with and overcome your waking-life fears. On another level, a lion can appear as your guardian, offering you protection and encouragement.

Make-up

Applying make-up in a dream is all about changing your image in real life. You may want to hide behind a "mask" because you're not happy with yourself or because you have a secret desire to attract a certain someone and are putting on a new, attractive face. If you are making your-self up as a clown in the dream, again, it's a mask. It could mean you're trying to make light of something, or to put on a happy face to conceal the fact that you're really unhappy underneath. In general, however, dreams about cosmetics are all about finding ways to boost self-confi-dence in real life.

Marriage

To dream of a wedding, or of a bride and bridegroom, is often wish-fulfillment, especially if you've recently been to a wedding. But take note of any strange additions in your dream, for this is where your message lies. What colors do you see? is it a white wedding? If you are getting married, it could mean you're about to strike up a new friendship or get together with someone else to work on a project.

Money

Is your dream about loss or gain? Receiving money is a great omen, since you will be given something of value in the near future. It may not necessarily be cash, but it could be a gift or compliment that is important to you. Finding money implies good luck, recognition or something good coming your way. Losing money suggests you'll lose something or you may break up with a friend. Counting money is a good sign reflecting harmony at home.

Moon

The ancient symbol of the moon stands for women and mothers, or for intuition and imagination. Dreams of the moon may be referring to your relationship with your mother or other female friends. A full moon says that all will be well in your daily life, with everything coming to fruition. Seeing a new moon means a new start. A moonlit

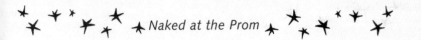
scene indicates that all may not be what it seems in your life. This dream is telling you to use your feelings and intuition before you make an important decision and to check some facts from the past.

Mother

If you have a good relationship with your mother, your dream will bring support and understanding. If you argue a lot, the dream may be reflecting some of that uncomfortable feeling. Fighting with your mother in your dream may be a warning about a disagreement with a female friend or other member of your family. Some good and helpful advice could be wrapped in this dream because the mother symbol is nurturing and caring.

Music

In whatever way you experience music in a dream, it brings the inspirational message that happiness and harmony are around you. Many famous composers and musicians have heard a tune in their dreams and written it up as soon as they awoke. If you are playing an instrument that you can't

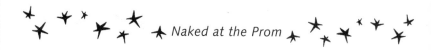
play in waking life, this could be a wish-fulfillment dream. But it could also be encouragement from your subconscious, telling you that you have the power to develop your hidden talents, musical or otherwise. To hear music or be listening to music in a dream implies you will soon be receiving some very good news.

Nudity

We all have this kind of dream at some time or other, usually when we're going through a period in our lives when we're lacking in confidence or have a fear of exposure. If in your dream you're walking down the street with no clothes on, it's all about embarrassment, fearing you're going to make a fool of yourself in real life, or that others will laugh at you. A dream where someone walks in on you naked shows that you're afraid of exposure, of "being found out," or of the "real you" coming out. This kind of dream may also be warning you not to give away too much information about yourself or, in other words, to not "let it all hang out."

Numbers

There is an ancient mystery and magic behind numbers, so when you dream of them it's a good idea to recall as much

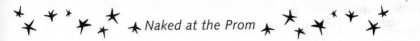

detail as you can. Of course, lots of people hope they'll dream of the winning lottery numbers, and some do! The trick is to remember them when you wake up. If you've been doing math homework before bed, it's likely you'll dream of numbers in some way. To dream of your address reflects an event involving your home and family. If you see your phone number, it means you'll hear from someone soon. Numbers are symbolically important and each one carries a different meaning, so the message of your dream will be found in whatever that number means.

One

In a dream, ONE can refer to your being "Number 1," like "I" or "myself." To dream of this may mean you need to establish your identity in waking life. Perhaps this dream is encouraging you to stand up for yourself, or to work harder so you can achieve something important in life. Alternatively, it could be warning you not to be so selfish or pushy. Number ONE holds the power of beginning and winning. It's the start of something new and holds the magic of untold possibilities.

Two

The number TWO symbolizes duality. It's the sign of a twosome – a couple of friends, boy-girl, man-wife. It also represents balance. In a dream, TWO can be highlighting a special friendship that may need to be

kept in balance with equal give and take. Alternatively, this dream may be reminding you to see the "other side of the coin" before making a decision.

Three

Three is the number of creativity and refers to your talents, style and self-expression. In a dream, the number THREE is encouraging you to develop your creative flair. But it is also the number of fun so is a sign that good things are going to happen. In folk and fairy tales people were often given three wishes. Perhaps this is what your dream is suggesting!

Four

The number FOUR is associated with self-discipline, responsibility and practical matters. To dream of this number, then, may be a prompt that you need to focus more on your work, or it may be reminding you of your duties. A good dream with the number FOUR in it says that you can achieve great things if you get yourself organized and get on with your work.

Five

Because FIVE represents adventure, dreaming of this number is an encouragement to try something new or to consider different options in your waking life. We have five senses, so the subconscious may be telling you to put all of them on alert, to shape up and get

your act together. When you dream of this number, your subconscious is telling you to be more experimental. Essentially, it's saying: go on, try it!

Six

SIX is a powerful number representing harmony, wisdom and knowledge. And because it is also the number of honesty and reliability, a dream with this number may be pointing to someone who is genuine and sincere. Your dream is telling you this is a person you can trust with your secrets, someone who can give you good advice if you have a problem.

Seven

A magical, mystery tour of a number, SEVEN contains both the spiritual and the physical. It's a rather high-brow concept but essentially SEVEN links in with your sensitivity to art, music and literature. If this number is significant in your dream, it's an encouragement to develop your skills in these fields. If in real life you tend to be a bit of a day-dreamer, this number may be telling you that it's time to be more practical and to come down to earth.

Eight

Just by writing the figure EIGHT you can feel its continuous flow, so in dreams it's telling you to go with the flow in real life. A dream in which this number is

prominent reassures you that you're in a lucky phase where everything is working perfectly. EIGHT is often connected with riches and wealth, so seeing this number in a dream may be a sign that good fortune is coming your way.

Nine

The number NINE is associated with caring and sharing, and dreaming about it means that either you'll be doing a kindness for someone in your waking life or someone will be doing something nice for you. NINE is the number of unselfishness, so if you see this number often in your dreams, it's reassuring you that you're a thoughtful and considerate person. However, if you know you're not, then this is your subconscious telling you to stop being so mean!

Ten

When you dream of the number TEN you're seeing the symbolism of unity, perfection and completion, so perhaps you have reached a well-earned goal after lots of hard work where everything has come together at last. TEN is the perfect number. It marks the satisfactory conclusion of some part of your life and now it means you can go forward with confidence. It's saying: you're moving on!

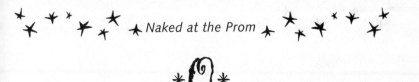
Offices

When you find yourself in an office-type dream it's referring to your routine in your daily life. If the office is a mess, perhaps it means you need to be more efficient and tidy with your schoolwork and assignments. Do you recognize the office? If it's where your mother works, the dream message could be about her. Anything special or unusual about the office, such as machinery, files or colors, will give you clues as to what the dream is all about. A copier, for example, may suggest you need to copy somebody's good example. Looking through files means there's something you need to check up on, or something you have to remember.

Orchards

Fruit trees have a cycle of annual growth, and in dreams the important phases are spring, when the blossom bursts through, and summer and autumn, when the fruit grows and ripens. What is the orchard like and what are you doing there? Blossom on fruit trees indicates a healthy promise for the future. The condition of the fruit on the trees is important. If green and unripe, then the opportunity you hoped for is going to take longer than anticipated. When the fruit is ripe and ready for picking, your ideas will be "fruitful."

Owls

When this wise old bird appears in your
dream it's reflecting not only wisdom
but experience and clarity of vision. It
may be encouraging you to sharpen
your wits and focus on a current
concern, bringing all your know-
how to bear on it. Perhaps you're
being a bit of a "night-owl" at the
moment and having some late nights. Allow "owl wisdom"
to speak to you. It's bringing you good advice.

Packages

Receiving a package in a dream generally indicates good
news or a nice surprise on the way. If, however, you find
the contents are unpleasant, it's a warning that you may
receive bad news. Packing up a box during a dream symbolizes getting rid of something: a bad habit, for example.
Here, your subconscious is encouraging you to clear away
stuff and prepare for a new start.

Parents

A dream featuring both your parents very often has to do
with feelings of security. You may have been worrying

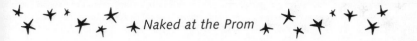

about them recently, or perhaps about having to leave them for a while. How they come across in the dream and how you feel will give you clues to the dream's meaning. A happy family scene confirms that your real life is content right now. Fights and disagreements, though, could reflect problems at home. (See also Father figures and Mother.)

Parties

Partying in a dream represents your current enjoyment of real life. If you are dancing and singing and are with happy people, it means life's going well and you have good opportunities to look forward to. If the dream party turns out to be weird rather than wonderful, it may be showing you that you're feeling left out of things or finding it difficult to relate to your friends at the moment in your waking life.

Pigs

No matter how you view them in real life, when you dream about a pig it's just not good news. It's all about behavior – either yours or someone else's – and the message points to selfishness, greediness or plain bad manners. If it's a male pig, which of course is a boar, the dream may be referring to someone who's being annoying or a bit of a "bore" in your life right now. Whatever the case, the pig is either a problem on the horizon or a reminder to improve your manners.

Presents – see Packages

Prisons

A dream about a prison or seeing yourself behind bars is usually a reference to a sense of isolation in real life. Being unable to find the key suggests you're trying to work out something in waking life but can't put your finger on the solution. Or perhaps it's suggesting you're trapped in a depressing situation. If you find the key it means you'll find the answer to your problem. (See also Keys and Zoos.)

Prizes

Being given a prize or a medal means you have either recently achieved something in real life or, if it's a predictive dream, you soon will. This is a positive dream where your subconscious is giving you a pat on the back and saying, "Well done!"

Quarrels

Dreaming that you're quarreling enables your mind to replay an argument you may have had recently in waking life, in order to release pent-up anger. Alternatively, a dream quarrel can symbolize a decision, being unsure which way to go and seeing both sides of the picture. (See also Fighting.)

Queens

A meeting with the Queen is a very fortunate omen in dreams and, according to research, most people will experience this dream at some time in their lives. It indicates that you can expect to be singled out for something special or will be lucky. It can also mark a turning point in your life. Should you find yourself part of the Queen's entourage, perhaps you have a longing to be noticed. If you yourself are a queen in your dream, this could be wish-fulfilling because maybe real life is boring right now and you are not getting the respect from others that you would like.

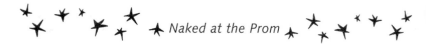
Quicksand

This is usually a nightmare situation where you feel yourself sinking deeper and deeper and can't escape. This dream may be reflecting feelings of insecurity and helplessness in some aspect of your waking life. Or perhaps it's telling you that you're getting into a situation too deep and should pull out before it's too late.

Races

The simple question here is, are you lagging behind or are you winning in the dream? Races usually describe our movement or the sort of progress we are making in life. So dreaming that you're taking part in a race may be your subconscious urging you to become more competitive, especially if you tend to be a little too laidback in waking life. If you're winning the race, it shows you're on top of things at the moment.

Chloe's dream

One night towards the end of the spring semester, Chloe dreamed she was in a race. The stadium

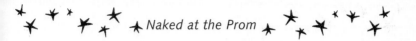

was packed and everyone was cheering for her. As
she took her place at the starting blocks she
looked around and realized she had some fierce
compe-tition. When the starter's gun fired she was
off
like a bullet. Though she ran like the wind, others
were matching her pace for pace. At times she
forged ahead and at other times she lagged
behind. But, putting on a final spurt, she just
managed to cross the line in front.

Next day at school when report cards were given
out, Chloe found she had the highest grades in
her class – she had, as her dream foretold, won
the race.

— 🕸 —

Rain

Getting soaking wet in a dream is like taking a shower in
waking life – it's a way of freshening up, but in dreams the
rain cleanses and washes away your fears, stress and anxieties. Should you experience being in a violent storm in the
dream, heed the warning that there is turbulence ahead. But
don't forget that after every storm there is calm, so this dream
is a good omen and points to a happy ending in real life.

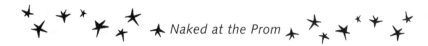

Rainbows

One of the best symbols to see in a dream, a rainbow holds the magic of true promise that new life is beginning. Your Dream Self is showing you that the storm has passed and your hopes for success and personal happiness in the future are the next phase. Take note if any one of the rainbow's colors is more prominent, because this color will carry a specific message. Look under Colors to add more depth to your analysis of this dream.

Rats

You may or may not like them in real life, but in dreams rats appear as a warning symbol. Who is behaving like a "dirty rat," going behind your back and telling on you, or making things up about you? The rat is the informer, the betrayer, so this dream is hinting that you may be let down by someone soon. A rat pack in the dream may be a warning that you're in with the wrong crowd.

Rivers

Dreaming of a river gives you information about how the course of your life is flowing right now, particularly regarding your feelings, because water symbolizes the emotions. Is the water clear or muddy; is it flowing gently or rapidly, or is it a rushing torrent? Muddy water equals confusion whereas clear water shows you're thinking clearly. If the

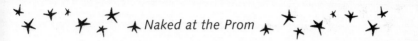

river is moving fast then your emotions may be veering out of control. A torrent suggests emotional turmoil, so you may be going through an upsetting time in waking life. If you see boulders or the river cascading over a waterfall, beware of arguments or disagreements! If you are in the river, struggling upstream, you may be having some difficulty with friends or family. If you are getting "out of your depth" in the water, watch out. This is definitely a warning that things are going wrong in your waking life.

Roads

A road in a dream indicates your journey in life: your past, present and future. When the road is smooth ahead, it's a sign that things are easy with no problems. Bumps, boulders, twists and turns, a poor stony surface or a fallen tree warn of obstacles and challenges that have to be overcome. The landscape the road passes through – pretty or rugged – will give further clues as to how your life is going at the moment. (See also Gardens.)

Rooms – see Houses

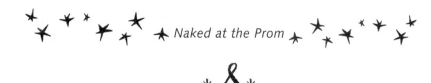

School

You may dream about your school if you're going through difficult times with friends, teachers or work, especially if there's been a particular real-life incident that's upset you. This type of dream is really a means by which your subconscious can release your feelings. It's also a way to bring things to your attention – perhaps something someone said that was important but you didn't quite catch – or your Dream Self is confirming a suspicion you may have about a school friend. Alternatively, this dream might be telling you there's something you need to learn, and life is about to teach you that lesson. (See also Classrooms and University.)

Scissors

Scissors in a dream generally mean cutting out or giving up something in waking life. This dream may be encouraging you to "cut out" a bad habit or "cut loose" from a person or situation. Dreaming that you're having your hair cut suggests you may need a new image. If someone is threatening you with scissors in a dream, it's a warning that a person you know in real life is jealous of you.

Sex

Dreams about sex are most often nature's way of releasing tension and emotion from our bodies. Because the sex urge is a fundamental part of who you are as a creative being, dreams about love and sex are natural and healthy. Dreams in which you're romantically involved with someone you like in real life, or with a favorite pop star, are often wishful thinking. If you dream you're male when in real life you're female, it's nature's way of asking you to recognize your "masculine" qualities of assertiveness and initiating action. If you're male and you dream that you're a female, it doesn't mean you should seek advice about a sex change. It's your Dream Self telling you to recognize your "feminine" qualities of nurturing and caring. Dreams about sex are very common and are usually healthy for mind, body and spirit.

Shoes

Shoes are a common theme in dreams because they easily reveal personal information about how we see ourselves and our progress. The condition of the shoes is a big clue to how you feel about yourself in real life. For example, if you're wearing nice new shoes, or if they're clean and well polished, it means you're feeling content and confident about things. If the shoes are old, scuffed or even falling apart,

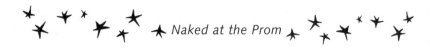
it could mean you're tired, fed up or that things are getting you down. Searching for shoes in a dream is warning you not to waste time in real life but get on with what you have to do! To lose shoes indicates you're fearful of taking the next step; you're unable to go forward in life. It might be wishful thinking when you have lots of pairs of shoes in the dream but it may also mean you're overdoing things and trying to be in too many places at the same time.

Smells

Dream researchers report that not many people dream about smells, and that real-life smells wafting into the bedroom while we are asleep, like perfume from the dressing table or bacon sizzling in the kitchen, will trigger a dream in which the smell is included. To experience a beautiful fragrance in your dream spells happiness and success. But take heed if the reverse happens and the dream smell is unpleasant. This is a warning that something fishy is going on in your waking life.

Snakes

Snakes and serpents share the same complex dream symbolism. Because of their phallic (penis-like) shape, these creatures are generally considered to represent the creative male force. However, when they are coiled they represent the feminine force. In dreams, a snake represents sexual

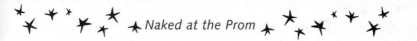
desire. It often appears in an erotic way if, say, you've been watching a sexy movie, or perhaps after you've met someone who really turns you on!

Spiders

Like them or loathe them, spiders are a good omen in dreams because they foretell good fortune. In ancient times the spider was known as the "weaver of destiny," spinning the web of creation. However, if in real life you're terrified of spiders, dreaming of one may be a warning that you have an enemy.

Sun

The sun is the ancient symbol for the masculine, the father principle (just as the moon is the symbol for the mother and feminine principle). We know the sun in the waking world as life force, light, power and energy, so if you see it shining in a dream it bodes well for you and your future plans. With this symbol your subconscious is telling you that you can't fail, that you're a winner. It's telling you to be confident because you're a star!

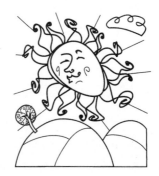

Teeth

Lots of people dream about teeth and there are several meanings that may apply. On the simplest level, such a dream could be reminder that you need to visit the dentist. A dream about losing teeth points to feelings of rejection or "losing face" in the waking world. This may be your Dream Self prompting you to assert yourself. If your teeth look bad in the dream it means a disappointment or a fight. But to dream of a beautiful row of even, white teeth means health, wealth and happiness await you in your waking life.

Telephones

If you dream about a telephone, it means news is on its way. If you can remember what is said, you'll have a clue as to what that news is going to be. If you answer the phone but can't make out what is being said, your Dream Self is telling you that you need to listen more to what others are trying to tell you in your waking life. If you see yourself chatting a lot, perhaps you're too talkative in class. If you're trying to call someone and can't get an answer, this hints that you're either finding it difficult to get in touch with your feelings or you think people aren't listening to you or aren't interested in your problems. This dream, then, is

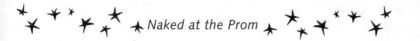

encouraging you to find a sympathetic friend who can be your special confidante – it could even be your mom.

Tests – see Exams

Theaters

Are you watching a performance or are you taking part? Either way, the symbolism of a theater is all about playing things out in the theater of life. What is being said, or the theme of the play you are watching, will give you clues to the meaning of your dream. If you are starring in the play, your subconscious is predicting that with a bit more self-confidence you could really shine. Being on a dream stage is all about recognition, so if in real life you're longing to be noticed, this dream is pointing you in the right direction.

Tigers

The symbology of the tiger includes power, strength and depth of vision, so a dream featuring this animal is connecting you to these characteristics and reinforcing your own abilities. Seeing the tiger's face, especially its eyes, means you need to be more watchful and aware of hidden factors before you make a judgement in your waking life. Tigers are dynamic, streamlined in action and full of energy, so be encouraged by this symbol to go for gold in your waking life.

Trains

Train dreams are common, signifying your journey through life and the present phase you're in. Getting onto a train in a dream signifies the start of a new phase in your life. If you're sitting down, it implies that you're relaxed about how things are going. But if you're standing or being jostled, it means you're having a bit of a struggle to keep your place in the scheme of things. If the train is crowded and people are pushing you, you're under pressure in your waking life. The items around you and the identity of the people hold the clues as to what or who is creating the problem.

Trees

A tree is an ancient symbol of dynamic life, strength and protection, and when it appears in a dream it is describing your life force. A tree that is bare of leaves is a reminder of winter – a time to conserve energy but to keep working quietly and persistently. If, however, your tree is a dead stump, it may be suggesting you're tired and low in spirits. You may have this dream when you're not well. To see a beautiful tree in full leaf shows you are in good health, thriving and creative. This is a very good omen to have in a dream. (See also Orchards.)

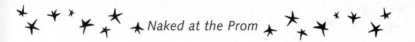

Tunnels

People often dream about tunnels. Sometimes, if you can't find your way out, this can be scary. It means that you're going through a difficult or confusing time in your waking life. Being in a tunnel and seeing a train coming towards you implies that in real life you're on a "collision course" with someone or with a certain situation. Seeing a light at the end of the tunnel means you will find a solution to your current problems. This is a positive dream, reassuring you that very soon you will "see the light." (See also Alleyways and Lights.)

Umbrellas

Think of the shape of an umbrella – how it provides protection and shelter from the rain. Water, don't forget, represents feelings, so the umbrella shows that whatever happens in your real life you have the power to rise above it and will be shielded against any difficulties that may arise. In this dream your subconscious is reassuring you that you can cope with whatever challenges lie ahead. If in your dream the umbrella is damaged, perhaps blown inside out, it is reflecting your insecurity at this time. Perhaps you're feeling vulnerable and in need of some protection or tender loving care.

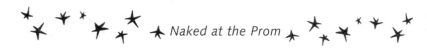

Underwear

A dream in which you are wearing only your underwear is reflecting your feelings of insecurity in waking life. Perhaps you are afraid of being "exposed" or you're feeling vulnerable about something. Generally, it reveals that you're feeling uncomfortable about a certain situation. (See also Embarrassment and Nudity.)

Uniforms (School)

School uniforms in our dreams represent rules and authority. If you're happy wearing the uniform, it means you're an obedient person who has no problems conforming to the situation. Dreaming that you're rebelling against wearing a uniform, however, shows either that you disagree with what's going on at the moment in your waking life or you're in conflict with someone in authority. This person could be a parent or a teacher at your school.

University (College)

A university is a place of learning, so to dream of one could imply you need to seek information about someone you

know or a project you're working on. Perhaps your subconscious is trying to tell you that you haven't got all the facts and you must go back and dig for more. On a more basic level, you may have this dream after you've been discussing college with friends or advisers. Your sleeping mind is then simply clearing out some of the images through this dream.

Vampires

Naturally, if you watch a horror movie before bed, images from it may well be released in such a dream. Since vampires are known for blood-sucking, if you have this dream you need to ask yourself who in your waking life may be draining your energy. Perhaps your best friend is very demanding of your attention, or your sister may be a terrible chatterbox so that by the end of the day you're left feeling drained and worn out. Or perhaps if you're involved in a lot of sports, this dream is making you realize how much all this activity is taking out of you.

Vegetables

Fresh vegetables pulsate with life so dreaming of a kitchen garden full of wonderful produce or a basket full of crisp cabbages, shiny peapods and bright orange carrots simply

confirms that you're brimming with health. If you see yourself eating vegetables, your subconscious may be telling you that you need to adopt a more nutritious diet. Rotting vegetables in your dream could be a sign that you're wasting your talents and potential. Consider some of the expressions we use: "couch potato," for example. This image may be telling you that you sit around too much and need to get more exercise. Or limp lettuce may be remarking on your lack of sparkle. Alternatively, it may be the color of the vegetable that's the important clue, like a red tomato or green spinach. Check out Colors to find the deeper levels of meaning that may be woven into this dream.

Volcanoes

The key word associated with this symbol is "erupting," so to dream of a volcano in action may be an indication that you need to "blow your top" over a situation that took place in the day. Alternatively, it may be a warning that someone you know is about to explode. One way or another, there is a lot of anger and frustration connected with this dream imagery.

W

Walking

The action of walking in a dream represents measured and steady movement towards your goal in waking life. It has a very similar meaning to other forms of travel – driving a car, riding a horse, cycling, or going on a train trip. All these different forms of movement show the progress you're making in your waking life. Should you encounter difficulties on your walk, such as struggling uphill or getting lost, it's a warning that difficulties – tests, for example – are coming up in your real life. If you're dawdling or you get side-tracked on your walk, your subconscious is telling you to stop dilly-dallying or wasting your time in waking life! If on your dream walk you stop to enjoy the pleasant view or take time to look at the flowers, it means that your life is interesting at the moment and you're enjoying what you're doing.

Walls

A wall can symbolize an obstacle or a boundary that is presenting a challenge to you in waking life. Interestingly, the wall could even represent a person who is blocking your way right now. If you find a way around the wall, or you manage to climb over it in your dream, then it bodes well because it means you will find a solution to whatever prob-

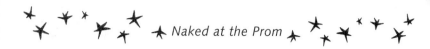

lems you may be experiencing at present in real life. (See also Fences.)

Washing – see Water

Water

In dreams, water represents the emotions, and it's the form and condition of the water that gives the clues as to the meaning of your dream. For example, diving out of a boat into the ocean may suggest you're "going overboard" for someone. Huge ocean waves crashing down over you implies you're being overwhelmed by your feelings. If the water is muddy and murky, your dream is telling you that you're confused and mixed up over a situation or someone you know. Washing yourself or your clothes in a dream denotes a desire to clean up your act and make a new start. Are you washing your hands? If so, it means you want to have nothing more to do with someone or something. To dream that you're drowning suggests things are seriously overwhelming you in waking life and you're finding it difficult to cope. If you're looking at a stagnant pond, your subconscious is telling you that your life is at a standstill and you need to develop new interests or make new friends. But to gaze over a calm lake or to be happily swimming in a warm, blue sea is a most positive message that life at present is fine, your emotions are well balanced and you're feeling happy and at ease.

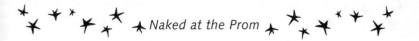

Windows

To dream that you're looking out of a window is a comment on your current view of life. If there are curtains in the way, it means you may not be seeing the situation clearly at present. The same message applies if you are looking through grimy windows. What do you see? A scene that occurred in the day will give you a chance to review what went on. To look out over a wonderful landscape indicates that life is going well and your future looks promising. If the scenery is rugged, there may be challenges ahead, perhaps problems with your friends or lots of revision to do. To see a brick wall in front of you suggests frustration; a mountain means hard work; people playing promises a fun time ahead. And if you see a pile of treasure, you could be coming into money soon.

Wolves

If a wolf appears to you in a dream, it is a positive image that shows protection, caring and healing. Symbolically a wolf is a great teacher who brings new ideas and information. But it all depends on what else is happening in your dream since a wolf can also be a warning of deceit and deception – as in the saying, "a wolf in sheep's clothing." If this is the image you see, watch out for someone you know who is not all he or she seems!

Woods – see Trees

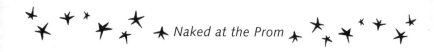

Youth

Interpretation here depends on the context. For example, to dream of a beautiful young man may be a yearning or wish-fulfillment dream, where you're longing to fall in love. Alternatively, you may be that youth, and what you're doing in the dream will be a comment on what's currently happening in your waking life. To see a group of young people may imply that you need to meet and mix with a new set of friends. Youth is a symbol of newness and freshness, so this image may be telling you it's time to start a new chapter in your life.

Zoos

A zoo hints that you're likely to be meeting new friends soon, very possibly from exotic countries. If you find yourself behind bars with a particular animal, who does that animal represent? Certain characteristics and similarities will remind you of a person you know in real life. Remember, to be "caged" in a dream, no matter what the circumstances, suggests you're feeling constricted or trapped in a waking life situation right now. (See also Animals.)

Magical Dreaming

Now let's take a look at the influence you the dreamer have on the dream itself. You see, because you're involved in the action of your dream, you have a direct influence on what happens. So, rather than thinking about dreams as something random, you can turn your dream into a creative and helpful experience. To do this you have to get your conscious, or waking-life, mind to work more fully with your subconscious. It's a process called Dream Incubation. It takes practice to perfect, but once you get the hang of it, you'll find the whole experience mind-blowing!

Four steps to dream incubation

1. What do you want your dream to tell you? Keep things simple to begin with and start with just one clear request. For example, you may need to find something you've lost. Or you may be seeking a solution to a difficult problem. Or else you might want to think up a winning slogan for that contest on the back of your cereal box.

2. Write down the simple question as if you were talking to your best friend because that's just what you are doing – you're communicating with your Dream Self.

3. You must read this over and over again and keep it in your mind during the day, and again as you get ready for bed. (By the way, don't do this exercise after watching a late-night movie.)

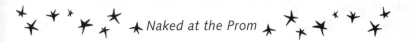

4. Once in bed, read over your question and ask your subconscious to bring you the answer during sleep. Then just relax and leave the whole thing to incubate. (Have your notebook and pencil ready by the bed!) What you're doing here is consciously programming yourself as the dreamer, giving your Dream Self this specific task. You need to focus your attention on a particular question because your subconscious is already busy with all the other dream work (such as off-loading problems) it has to do for you each night to keep you healthy and sound of mind.

You can use this same four-step technique in another way. Instead of a question, you can think up a place that you'd like to dream about – perhaps somewhere you've enjoyed a vacation or a favorite area anywhere in the world. Write down a simple description and the name of the place. Start at step 3, and in step 4 ask your subconscious to reflect the place in a positive, harmonious dream.

Helping your dreams come true

Your Dream Self operates in a timeless zone, so something you dreamed when you were very little may not come through into waking life until many years later. Often, it's not until you reach that point that you remember you had dreamed this all those years ago. At that time, it was probably a wish-fulfillment dream. For example, during a wonderful tropical vacation you might have wished you could live by the sea forever and then had a wonderful dream where you were living near the beach with your family. If, years later, you find yourself moving into a house by the sea, in a strange way, your dream has come true!

This gives rise to a little warning – whatever you wish for may come true, so be very careful and concise with your instructions to your Dream Self!

Wish-fulfillment dreams come about from day-dreaming in a "what if …" kind of way. Day-dreaming – constructive daydreaming, of course, not just being vacantly switched off! – has a very important place in helping dreams come true.

Pondering, thinking things through, constructing and creating are all ways of day-dreaming where you bring

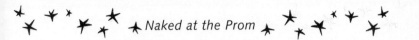

something into manifestation – the plot of a story, a plan for a vacation, inspiration for a painting, and so on. Creative day-dreaming links you into your Dream Self while you are awake. Another way to do this is through visualization or meditation when you let your thoughts drift into the deeper levels of your mind so that you can tap the inspiration of your subconscious.

So when it comes to helping your dreams come true, your greatest asset is your imagination. You imagine something – create a picture of it as perfectly as you know how – and using the four-step technique you instruct your Dream Self to reflect this wish in a dream and help you dream the dream while awake. In other words, you guide or manifest it into waking life. There can be no guarantee when this will happen, of course, but once you have set everything in motion it will usually come about in the most unexpected way.

To avoid an overload of the unexpected, please be careful! The following example is a true story.

A young woman fervently wished for the latest model of a certain car to be delivered to her house. Shortly afterwards, it arrived unexpectedly, crashing through her front window. She had neglected to be specific when creating the sequence of pictures in her dream wish.

The young woman should first have imagined the new car, then visualized the car keys being formally presented to her.

Finally, she should have staked her rightful claim to the car by sitting in the driver's seat and driving the vehicle away.

If your wishes involve material things, you have to set up the structure through which they can flow. Obviously, if you want to win the lottery you have to buy a ticket, and to win a contest you have to enter. And if you are flippant or greedy you are unlikely to get what you wish for.

Choosing your dream color

Go back to the entry on Colors in the A–Z section to remind you what each color means. Colors are powerfully therapeutic and visualizing them can bring you many benefits.

- A helpful tip if you're unhappy or unwell is to imagine green. It's Nature's color for soothing and healing. As you're settling down to sleep, imagine you're in a beautiful garden lying in a hammock under the trees, surrounded by lush green vegetation and green velvety lawns. Breathe in the green of the trees, the leaves and the lawn and then let green wrap itself around you like a soft cover as you go to sleep. Keep thinking and breathing green. Your body's natural healing processes will be encouraged and energized and you'll awaken in the morning feeling refreshed and restored.

- If you want to attract happiness and good fortune into your life, imagine you're standing at the end

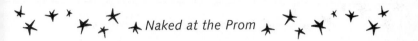

(or beginning) of a rainbow as it touches a green field. Stand right in the middle of it and let the colors shimmer around you. This time, the trick is to breathe in all seven colors – red, orange, yellow, green, blue, indigo and violet. You don't have to do them one by one, just know you're "breathing in a rainbow." In this way you'll be immersed in its magic and will absorb all the rainbow's benefits as you gradually fall asleep. You may even go on to dream you find the pot of gold.

• Violet, the color of the 21st century, can be imagined if you want to bring your life back into harmony. Perhaps you've had an argument or something depressing has happened, or you're just not feeling great. Dreaming with this color will transform any uneasy feelings and anxieties. Settle down for sleep and imagine you're surrounded by one of the lovely shades of violet – lavender is a good start. Start to breathe it in. If you find it difficult to imagine, just think of the plant itself. Keep breathing it in for around seven breaths, and as you breathe out imagine all the stress leaving your body. Then snuggle down and bring the pale violet color all around you as if you're in a cocoon. While you sleep, healing harmony will be working for you as if by magic. How easy can it be!

Now take a look at the other colors in the A–Z section and create your own scenarios just before drifting off to sleep.

Lucid dreaming

In lucid dreaming you are dreaming but you actually know you're having a dream! When that happens you are likely to experience more vivid colors and there will be a vibrant quality to the dream. Your dream is so much more real.

You also realize that you can control the dream. This is the key element of lucid dreaming – it's like creating a story or a scene in your imagination when you're awake.

True lucid dreaming is much more than a vague, fleeting awareness that a dream is taking place. You are able to hold onto and expand the experience by taking part in the action and deciding what that action will be.

You can control situations, reinvent endings and replay anything over and over until you've explored various possibilities. Your subconscious is helping you understand that you have choices in waking life and that you are in charge in order to achieve the best outcome – even while you sleep.

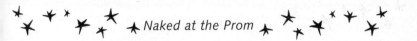

Not everyone is able to have lucid dreams. It takes a bit of practice but once you find the technique, it's well worth the effort.

You're more likely to have this type of dream first thing in the morning when you're in a very light sleep – after the alarm clock has roused you but you've drifted off again for 10 minutes. So one tip to induce a lucid dream is to set your alarm for 15 minutes earlier than usual to give yourself the chance to snooze again.

The alternative, and this is perhaps your best shot, is to have a nap at some point during the day. More people experience lucid dreaming when they're catching 40 winks mid-afternoon. As you settle down for your nap, instruct your subconscious to go into "lucid dream state." Tell your Dream Self there's a problem you need to figure out, or a situation you want to understand better. Keep thinking about this as you drift off.

At first, you'll start to have a normal dream, but then the dream will change and you'll think you've woken up. You haven't, of course; you're still in dream state but it really feels as if you're awake. It's at this point that you can start taking control. Now you can set the scene you want and call in the people who will help you resolve your problem or give you new insights into whatever is troubling you.

Don't be surprised if when you eventually wake up after a lucid dream you're a bit confused as to whether you're still dreaming or actually now awake for real! Just lie quietly to assimilate what you've discovered. You'll find it's quite an eye-opener.

A magical wonderland

Whether your dreams are lucid, precognitive, wish-fulfilling or just plain factual, they will all take you into a magical wonderland with layers of meaning that can keep you gripped for days trying to unravel and understand them. And in understanding your dreams, you will reach a better understanding of yourself.

Just remember, you are the dreamer, doing the dreaming and enacting the dream. Enjoy them all and make each one your best blockbuster yet!

May all your dreams
be wonderful
and may all your
wonderful dreams
come true.